A · SHORT · COURSE · IN NIKON · PHOTOGRAPHY

REVISED EDITION

P9-CAL-987

· A Guide to Great Pictures ·

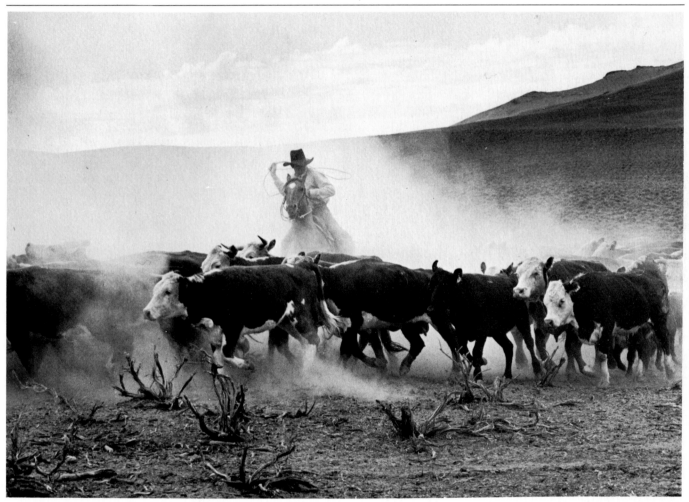

Carl Fleischhauer

· BARBARA LONDON ·

Curtin & London, Inc.
Somerville, Massachusetts

Van Nostrand Reinhold Company
New York · Cincinnati · Toronto · Melbourne

Printed in the United States of America

Published in 1983 by Curtin & London, Inc. and Van Nostrand Reinhold Company 135 West 50th Street, New York, NY 10020, U.S.A.

Van Nostrand Reinhold Limited
1410 Birchmount Road
Scarborough, Ontario M1P 2E7, Canada

Van Nostrand Reinhold Pty. Ltd.
17 Queen Street
Mitcham, Victoria 3132, Australia

Acknowledgments

Thank you to those organizations who granted us permission to reproduce the photographs on the following pages: Bethlehem Steel, 103 (bottom); EPA - Documerica, 5 (top), 24, 29 (top), 59, 63 (top), 72, 82, 85, 103 (top); Library of Congress American Folklife Center, i, 9 (center), 67 (bottom), 84, 99, 109 (bottom), 113 (top and bottom, left), 115 (top and bottom, right); National Park Service, 9 (top), 28, 32, 50, 63 (bottom), 67 (top), 69 (bottom), 71 (bottom), 74, 97 (top); U.S. Department of Agriculture, 22, 23, 26, 34 (top), 38, 43 (top and bottom), 44, 45, 49, 52 (top and bottom), 57, 62, 66, 70 (right), 73, 87 (top left, top right, and bottom), 96, 101, 104, 105 (top and bottom), 107 (top and bottom), 110 (left), 111 (top), 112 (top), 113 (bottom right), 115 (bottom left); Nikon, Inc., 116–132.

Cover design and interior design: Richard Spencer
Cover photograph: R. Ingo Riepl
Illustrations: Carol Keller
Production editor: Alison Fields
Composition: Jay's Publishers Services, Inc.
Printing and binding: Halliday Lithograph
Color insert printed by: Phoenix Color Corp.

Library of Congress Cataloging in Publication Data
London, Barbara
  A short course in Nikon photography.

  Includes index.
  1. Nikon camera. 2. Photography—Handbooks, manuals, etc. I. Title.
  TR263.N5U67 1983   771.3'1   83–5277
  ISBN 0–930764–54–4

10 9 8 7 6 5 4 3 2 1

· CONTENTS ·

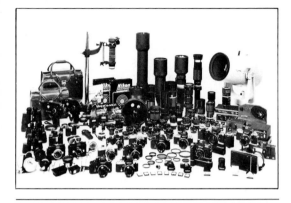
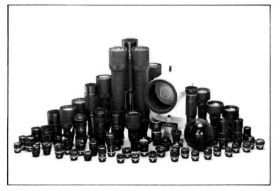

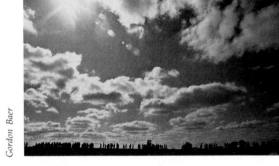

Gordon Baer

· CHAPTER 3 ·

Film and exposure · 38

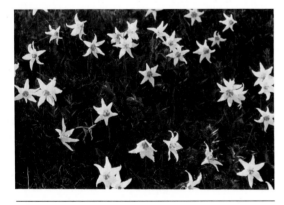

· CHAPTER 4 ·

Color · 60

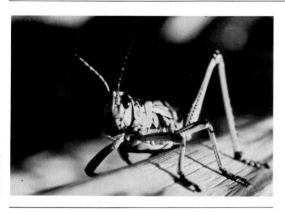

Fred Ward

· CHAPTER 5 ·

Special techniques · 72

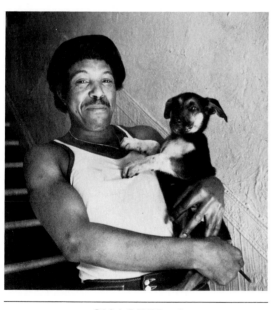

Jonas Dovydenas

· CHAPTER 6 ·

Lighting · 84

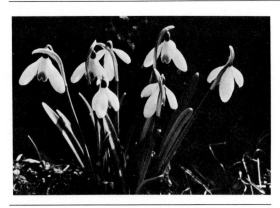

· CHAPTER 7 ·

Seeing like a camera · 96

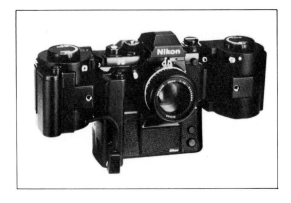

Guide to Nikon equipment and accessories · 116

· PREFACE ·

Camera controls—f-stops, shutter speeds, focal length of lenses, focusing—can initially appear to be very complicated. But if you have just bought or are contemplating the purchase of a modern 35mm single-lens-reflex camera, all that you need to know to begin taking good pictures can be learned in a weekend and probably on a Saturday afternoon. The key is that the basic principles that take this short amount of time to learn have an almost infinite variety of combinations and it is those combinations that make photography both interesting and an avocation with a lifetime of possible growth.

Photography isn't as difficult as it used to be. The innovations in equipment make it much easier to get good exposures in all kinds of lighting situations. The introduction of new materials and electronic technology, particularly computer circuitry, have made possible a new generation of cameras—simple to operate, compact, and versatile. Today, you can master the basics much faster, so you can concentrate on what is important . . . the image.

This book covers the basic principles of photography, the ones that must be understood to take full advantage of the creative controls on the camera you use. Essentially you need to know how to obtain a good exposure and how to use focus, aperture (the size of the lens opening), and shutter speed to create the picture you want. These basic principles are stressed and presented completely. In addition, the book covers film, flash, exposure meters, accessory equipment, and other important information.

The book is designed so that every two facing pages complete a fundamental idea. This format permits you to use the book as a reference and to learn about specific topics as the need arises. The book is heavily illustrated with photographs and line art so that it can be understood more easily and quickly. It has been completely revised and updated in this brand-new edition to bring you the latest information on camera equipment and accessories.

There is no doubt that greater satisfaction comes from using the camera as a creative tool and it is toward that end that this book will lead. ▪

Chapter 1
· THE NIKON CAMERA ·

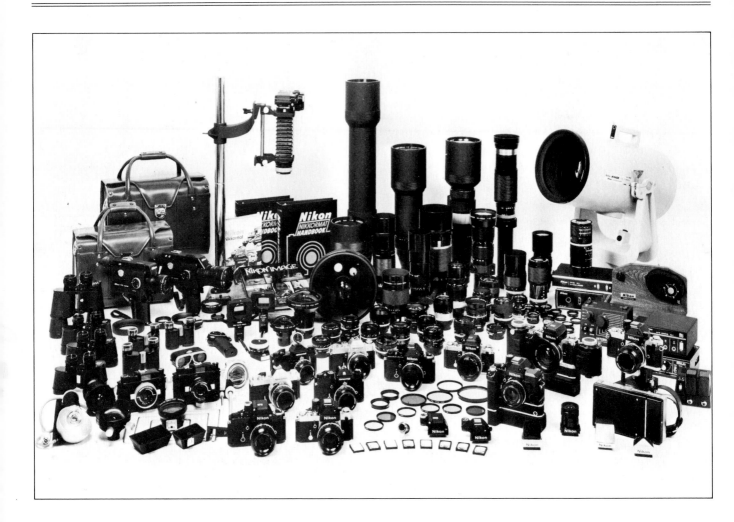

If you have progressed beyond the stage of simply wanting to take ordinary snapshots, then a Nikon 35mm single-lens-reflex (SLR) is an excellent camera for you to use. It is small enough to carry almost anywhere yet it uses film large enough to produce prints and slides of good quality. The special features and great flexibility of Nikon SLRs make them popular with professional photographers, with people who are seriously interested in photography, and with those who like to take pictures just for the fun of it.

Through-the-lens viewing A single-lens-reflex uses the same lens both for viewing the scene and for exposing the film, so what you see in the camera's finder is a good indication of what you'll get in the final picture. With a built-in exposure meter you can measure the brightness of the scene directly through the lens in order to determine how much to expose the film. And you can do this while looking at the exact area or object that is being metered.

Automation In just the last few years a revolution has occurred in camera design. In many models one of the major controls in picture making—exposure—has been taken over by tiny silicon chips and other components built into the camera. This electronic circuitry measures the light and then lets in just enough to expose the film properly. In some cases you will want to (and you usually can) override the decision of these automatic calculators, but in many situations they will expose your picture so well that all you have to do is focus and shoot. And for the maximum in auto-

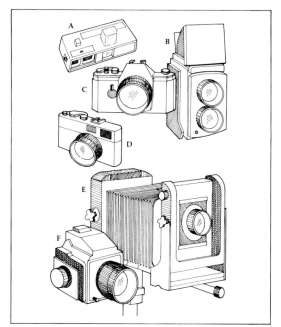

(A) pocket camera
(B) twin-lens-reflex
(C) 35mm single-lens-reflex
(D) 35mm range finder
(E) 4 × 5 view camera
(F) large format single-lens-reflex

mation, some cameras will confirm your focus or even focus automatically for you.

Compact size When you hold a Nikon 35mm single-lens-reflex camera in your hands, it feels comfortable—compact and convenient to carry with you. SLRs are getting even smaller and lighter as electronic circuitry replaces the maze of springs and gears that used to power shutters and other mechanisms.

Versatility When you buy a Nikon SLR, you are buying a system, not just a camera. Lenses are interchangeable and certain other parts are as well. Options like automatic flash units and motor-driven film advance are available.

This book describes Nikon SLRs and tells you how you can use their special features to make the pictures you want. ▪

USING YOUR NIKON'S
BASIC CREATIVE CONTROLS

Cameras don't quite "see" the way the human eye does, so at first the pictures you get may not be the ones you expected. One of the aims of this book is to help you gain control over the picture-making process by showing you how to see more the way the camera does and how to use the camera's controls to make the kind of pictures you want. ▪

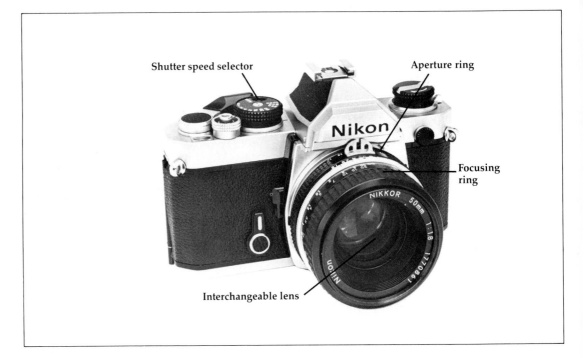

Shutter speed selector

Aperture ring

Focusing ring

Interchangeable lens

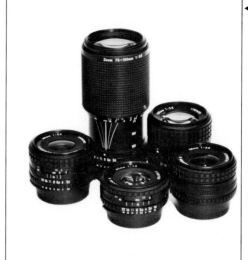

◄ **Interchangeable lenses** With a single-lens-reflex you can make a picture with a lens of normal focal length—a lens that views a scene just about as you do. Or, since you can carry several lenses with you and change them as you wish, you can get very different pictures of the same scene—a greatly enlarged image of a distant object, for example. See opposite, bottom and pages 20–27 for more about focal lengths. ▶

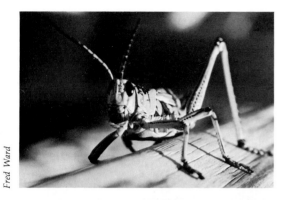

Fred Ward

Focusing Through the viewfinder window you see the scene that will be exposed on the film, including the sharpest part of the scene, which is the part the camera is focusing on.

A particular part of a scene can be focused sharply by turning the focusing ring on the lens. More about focusing and sharpness appears on pages 12–15 and 30–33.

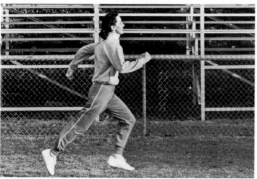
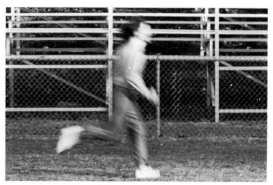

Alan Oransky

Shutter speed control Objects that are moving can be shown dead sharp and frozen in mid-motion or blurred, either a little bit or a lot. Turn to pages 10–11 and 14–15 for information about shutter speeds, motion, and blur.

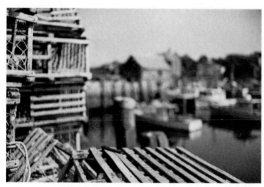
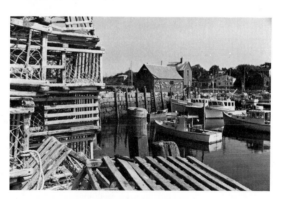

Fredrik D. Bodin

Aperture control Do you want part of the picture sharp and part out of focus, or do you want the whole picture sharp from foreground to background? Changing the size of the aperture (the lens opening) is one way to control this. More about aperture on pages 12–15.

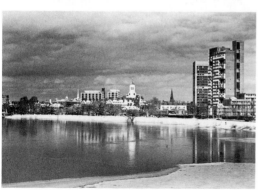
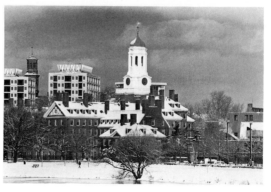

Alan Oransky

INSIDE A 35mm
SINGLE-LENS-REFLEX

The lightweight, compact body of a modern single-lens-reflex camera is sleek and functional. If you could cut away the shell of your SLR, you'd find packed inside thousands of precisely engineered mechanical and electronic parts. All of them are there to help you take better pictures—by making the camera easy to operate, critically accurate in focusing and other controls, and rugged enough to be reliable day after day. Below is a simplified look inside a single-lens-reflex (designs vary in different models). The camera takes its name from its single lens (some reflex cameras have two lenses) and from its reflection of light upwards for viewing the image. ∎

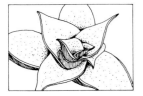 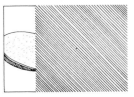 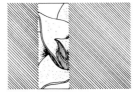 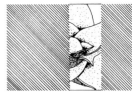 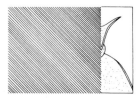

The shutter of a single-lens-reflex camera is located just in front of the film (at L in the camera diagram). During exposure the shutter opens to form a slit that moves across the film. The size of the slit is adjustable; the wider the slit, the longer the exposure time and the more light that reaches the film. Shown here is a shutter that travels horizontally across the film. Some shutters travel vertically.

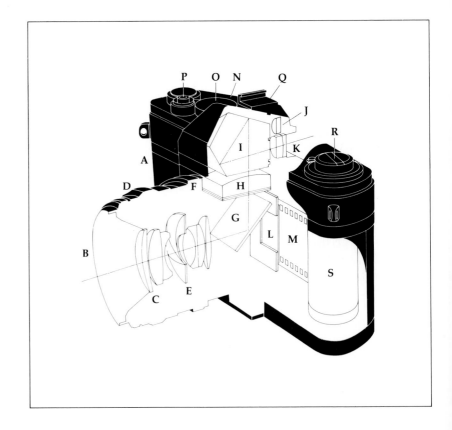

Inside a single-lens-reflex (opposite)

A. Body The light-tight box that contains the camera's mechanisms and protects the film from light until you are ready to make an exposure.

B. Lens Focuses an image on the film. Single-lens-reflex lenses are interchangeable.

C. Lens elements The optical glass lens components that produce the image.

D. Focusing ring Turning the ring focuses the image by adjusting the distance of the lens elements from the film plane.

E. Iris diaphragm A circle of overlapping leaves that open up to increase (or close down to decrease) the amount of light reaching the film.

F. Aperture ring Turning the ring adjusts the size of the iris diaphragm inside the lens.

G. Mirror During viewing, the mirror reflects light from the lens upwards onto the viewing screen.

H. Viewing screen A ground-glass (or similar) surface on which the focused image appears upside down and backwards. Some SLR cameras have interchangeable viewing screens with cross lines or other features.

I. Pentaprism A five-sided optical device that reflects the image from the viewing screen until it appears right side up and correct from left to right. On some cameras the pentaprism can be replaced with a specialized viewfinder such as a waist-level finder.

J. Metering cell Measures the brightness of the scene being photographed.

K. Viewfinder eyepiece A window in which the corrected image from the pentaprism is visible to the photographer.

L. Shutter During an exposure, the mirror first swings upwards out of the way so the light passes straight ahead. Then the shutter opens to expose the film to the light. Shutter action is diagrammed opposite at top.

M. Film The light-sensitive material that records the image.

N. Film advance A lever that advances an unexposed segment of film behind the shutter in preparation for exposure.

O. Shutter speed dial Selects the shutter speed or, in some models, the mode of automatic exposure operation.

P. Shutter release A button that activates the exposure sequence in which the mirror rises, the shutter opens, and the film is exposed.

Q. Hot shoe A bracket that attaches a flash unit to the camera and with suitable units provides the electrical linking that synchronizes the camera and the flash.

R. Rewind mechanism A crank that rewinds the film into its cassette after the roll of film has been exposed.

S. Film cassette The light-tight container in which 35mm film is packaged.

NIKON SLR ELECTRONICS

As cameras become more complex internally, incorporating sophisticated computing modules and other electronic devices, they are actually becoming *less* complicated for the photographer to use. One of the advantages of the new camera electronics is that you can spend more time concentrating on the people or location you are photographing and less time making exposure readings and calculations.

You have a choice of exposure modes with some cameras. The Nikon FE features aperture-priority automation. In its automatic mode you set the size of the aperture (lens opening) and the camera automatically sets the correct shutter speed (from 8 seconds to 1/1000 second) for proper exposure. Since you choose the aperture, you have creative control of the depth of field or sharpness of the image, because the size of the lens opening is a major factor affecting sharpness.

Manual operation is also possible with the FE. You set both the lens opening and shutter speed yourself, using, if you wish, the camera's built-in light meter to measure the brightness of the light. More information about the FE appears on page 118. ▪

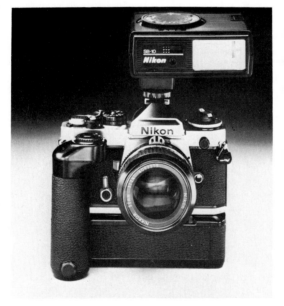

The Nikon FE compact automatic, 35mm single-lens-reflex camera with the Nikon SB-10 Electronic Flash and MD-12 Motor Drive.

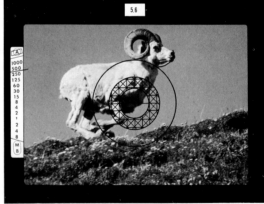

The FE's viewfinder constantly displays exposure information so you can keep your eye on your subject. Shutter speeds are shown on the vertical bar at left and the selected aperture appears above. When using the SB-10 flash unit, a flash-ready light in the viewfinder lets you know when the flash is fully charged and ready to use.

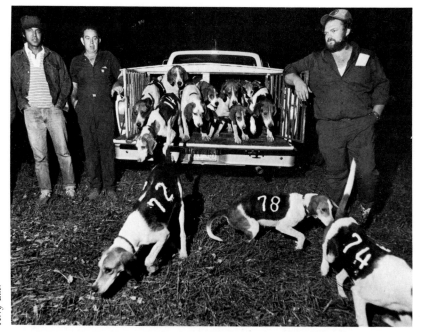

Terry Eiler

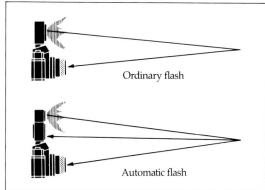

Ordinary flash

Automatic flash

For flash pictures the SB-10 Auto Speedlight automatically sets the FE to the correct shutter speed for flash synchronization. A sensor on the flash reads the light re-flected back from the subject and cuts off the flash at the prop-er exposure. See pages 128–129 for more about Nikon flash units.

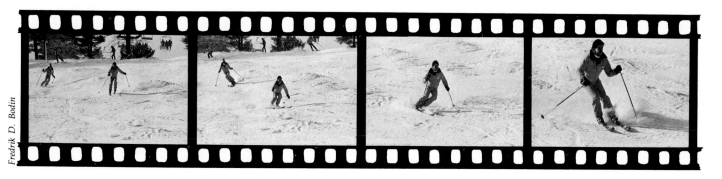

Fredrik D. Bodin

The MD-12 Motor Drive advances and exposes film with one push of a button. It can capture sequences of photographs at speeds up to 3.5 frames per second or will advance and ex-pose the film a single frame at a time.

SHUTTER SPEED:
AFFECTS LIGHT AND MOTION

Light and the shutter speed The shutter is one way to control the amount of light that strikes the film. (The aperture, page 12, is the other.) The shutter speed dial on the camera sets the shutter so it remains open for a given fraction of a second after the shutter release is pressed (see illustration below). The B, or bulb, setting keeps the shutter open as long as the shutter release is held down.

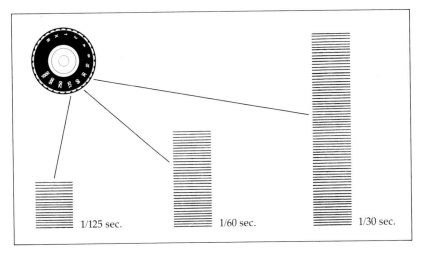

1/125 sec.　　1/60 sec.　　1/30 sec.

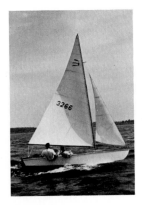
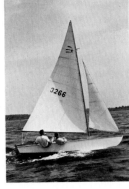
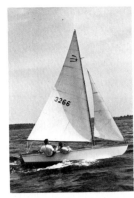

Motion and the shutter speed In addition to controlling the amount of light that enters the camera, the shutter speed also affects the way that moving objects are shown. A fast shutter speed can freeze motion—from a ballet leap to a falling drop of water. A slow shutter speed keeps the lens open long enough for the image to blur. The important factor is how much the image actually moves across the film. The more of the film it crosses while the shutter is open, the more the image will be blurred. The shutter speed needed to freeze motion depends in part on the direction in which the subject is moving in relation to the camera (see opposite).

The focal length of the lens and the distance of the subject from the camera also affect the size of the image on the film and thus how much it will blur. A subject can appear small if it is photographed with a short-focal-length lens or if it is far from the camera, and so it may move relatively far before its image crosses enough of the film to be blurred.

Obviously, the speed of the motion is also important, and, all other things being equal, a darting swallow needs a faster shutter speed than a hovering hawk. Even a fast-moving subject, however, may have a peak in its movement, when the motion slows just before it reverses. A gymnast at the height of a jump, for instance, or a motorcycle on a sharp curve is moving slower than at other times and so can be sharply photographed at a relatively slow shutter speed.

Shutter speed settings are typically in seconds: 1 sec., 1/2 sec., 1/4, 1/8, 1/15, 1/30, 1/60, 1/125, 1/250, 1/500, 1/1000, and sometimes 1/2000 and 1/4000. Only the bottom part of the fraction appears on the shutter speed dial and in any exposure information displayed in the viewfinder. Each setting lets in twice as much light as the following setting (or half as much as the previous setting): 1/60 sec. lets in twice as much light as 1/125 sec., half as much as 1/30 sec.

Blurring to show motion Freezing a motion is one way of representing it, but not the only way. In fact, freezing a motion sometimes eliminates movement altogether so that the subject seems to be at rest. Allowing the subject to blur can be a graphic means of showing that it is moving.

Panning to show motion Panning the camera—moving it in the same direction as the subject's movement during the exposure—is another way of showing motion (bottom right). The subject will appear sharper than it would if the camera were held steady, while the background will be blurred. ▪

1/30 sec.

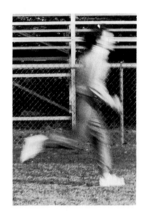

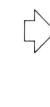

1/125 sec.

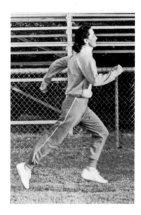

Slow shutter speed, subject blurred The direction a subject is moving in relation to the camera can affect the sharpness of the

picture. At a slow shutter speed, a jogger moving from left to right is not sharp.

Fast shutter speed, subject sharp Photographed at a faster shutter speed, the same jogger moving in the same direc-

tion is sharp. During the shorter exposure her image did not cross enough of the film to blur.

1/30 sec.

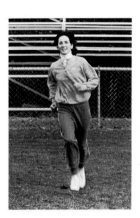

1/30 sec.

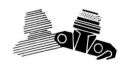

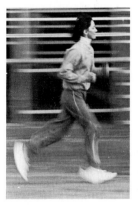

Alan Oransky

Slow shutter speed, subject sharp Here the jogger is sharp even though photographed at the slow shutter speed that recorded blur in the

first picture. Because she was moving directly toward the camera, her image did not cross enough of the film to blur.

Panning with the jogger is another way to keep her relatively sharp. During the exposure the photographer moved the

camera in the same direction that the jogger was moving.

APERTURE: AFFECTS LIGHT AND DEPTH OF FIELD

Light and the aperture The aperture, or lens opening, is another control that you can use in addition to shutter speed to adjust the brightness of the light that reaches the film. Turning a ring on the outside of the lens changes the size of the aperture diaphragm, a ring of overlapping metal leaves inside the lens. Like the iris of your eye, the diaphragm can get larger (open up) to let more light in; it can get smaller (stop down) to decrease the amount of light.

Light and the aperture The size of the lens opening—the aperture—controls the amount of light that passes through the lens. Each aperture is one "stop" from the next, that is, each lets in twice as much light as the next smaller opening, half as much light as the next larger opening. Notice that the smaller the lens opening, the larger the numeral. F/22 is a smaller opening than f/16, which is smaller than f/11, and so on.

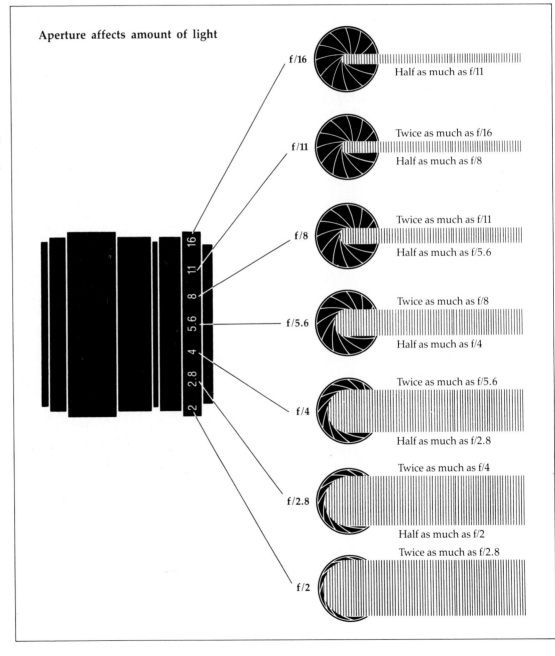

Aperture affects amount of light

f/16 Half as much as f/11

f/11 Twice as much as f/16
      Half as much as f/8

f/8   Twice as much as f/11
      Half as much as f/5.6

f/5.6 Twice as much as f/8
      Half as much as f/4

f/4   Twice as much as f/5.6
      Half as much as f/2.8

f/2.8 Twice as much as f/4
      Half as much as f/2

f/2   Twice as much as f/2.8

Aperture setting (f-stops) These are: f/1 (theoretically the widest opening), f/1.4, f/2, f/2.8, f/4, f/5.6, f/8, f/11, f/16, f/22, f/32, f/45. F-stops smaller than f/45 are seldom found. Each aperture setting lets in twice as much light as the next setting up the scale (or half as much light as the next setting down the scale). The relationship is not as obvious from the sequence of f-stop numbers as it is with shutter speeds (which also have a half-or-double relationship: 1 second, ½ second, ¼ second, and so on), but after a while the f-stops become just as familiar and easy to remember. No lens has the entire range of f-settings. A 50mm lens may range from f/2 to f/16, a 200mm lens from f/4 to f/22.

One irregularity sometimes occurs: the widest f-stop may be slightly less or slightly more than one full stop from the next setting. For example, a lens may open to f/3.5, then go to the regular sequence of f/4, f/5.6, and so on.

Depth of field and the aperture The size of the aperture setting also affects the relative sharpness of objects in the image, known as depth of field. In theory, only one distance from the lens, the plane of critical focus, can be acutely focused at one time. However, in practice, part of the scene near the plane of critical focus also appears acceptably sharp. As the aperture opening gets smaller, the depth of field increases and more of the scene appears sharp in the photograph. (More about depth of field on pages 30–33.) ▪

Aperture affects depth of field

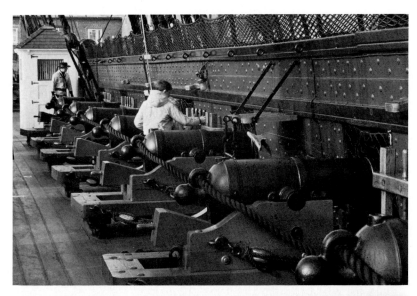

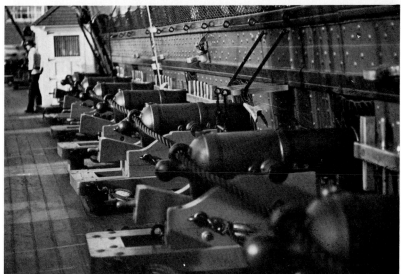

Fredrik D. Bodin

Depth of field and the aperture The larger the aperture opening, the less the depth of field. At f/16 (above) the entire depth in the scene from foreground to background was sharp. At a much larger aperture, f/2 (below), the depth of field decreased considerably so that only the third cannon from the front, on which the photographer focused, is completely sharp.

SHUTTER SPEED AND APERTURE: BLUR VS. DEPTH OF FIELD

Controlling the amount of light
There are two controls over the amount of light striking the film: shutter speed (length of exposure) and aperture (brightness of light). Either one can be used to increase or decrease the amount of light.

Each f-stop setting lets in half (or double) the amount of light as the adjoining setting. Each shutter speed setting does the same. A move to the next setting changes the exposure by one stop. Correct exposure can be obtained from any combination of f-stop and shutter speed settings that lets in the proper amount of light. The exposure stays constant if, for example, a move to the next faster shutter speed (minus one stop exposure) is matched

by a move to the next larger aperture (plus one stop exposure).

Other effects on the image But since the shutter speed also affects the way motion is shown and the size of the aperture also affects the overall sharpness of the photograph (its depth of field), you can decide for each picture whether stopped motion or depth of field is more important. More depth of field (with a small aperture) means more possibility of blur (with a slow shutter speed) and vice versa. Depending on the situation, you may have to compromise on a moderate amount of depth of field with some possibility of blur. ▪

Shutter speed and aperture combinations Both the shutter speed and the aperture size control the amount of light that strikes the film. Each setting lets in half (or double) the amount of light as the adjacent setting. In manual exposure operation (where you set both the shutter speed and aperture), changing from one setting to the next changes the exposure by one stop, so if you decrease the amount of light one stop by moving to the next smaller f-stop setting, you can keep the exposure constant by

also moving to the next slower shutter speed.

In automatic exposure operation, the camera makes these adjustments for you. For example, if you change the aperture, the camera automatically changes the shutter speed to keep the exposure constant.

Each combination of f-stop and shutter speed shown lets in the same amount of light, but, as illustrated at right, different f-settings and shutter speeds change the depth of field and appearance of motion in the picture.

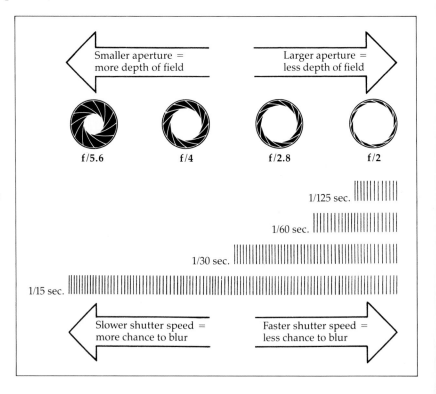

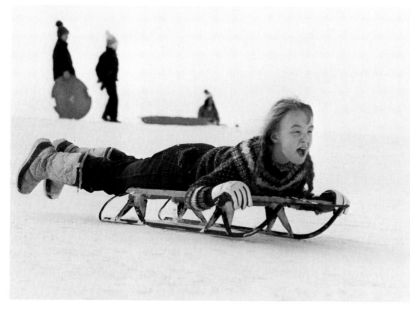

Shutter speed and aperture combinations Each of the combinations for the scene at left let in the same total amount of light, so the overall exposure stayed the same. But the people sledding are less or more blurred depending on whether a fast or slow shutter speed was used. And the depth of field (overall sharpness of nonmoving objects) is greater or smaller depending on whether a small or large aperture was used.

Very fast shutter speed (1/1000 sec.): the sled and rider are sharp. **Very wide aperture** (f/2): the people in the background are definitely out of focus.

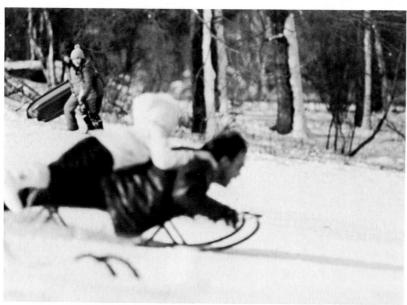

Medium-fast shutter speed (1/125 sec.): the moving sled is slightly blurred. **Medium-wide aperture** (f/5.6): the background is sharper than above.

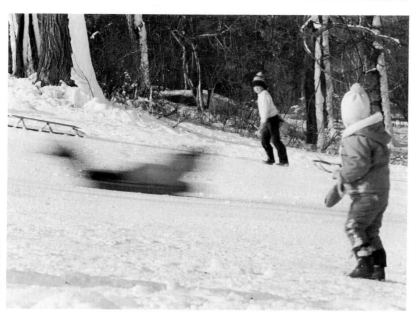

Slow shutter speed (1/15 sec.): the sled is very blurred because of its motion during the exposure. **Small aperture** (f/16): the trees are distinctly sharp; compare the branches to the picture above.

CARE OF
CAMERA AND LENS

Cameras are remarkably sturdy instruments considering the precision mechanisms that they contain, but a reasonable amount of care in handling and maintaining a camera will more than repay you with longer trouble-free life and better performance.

To protect a camera in use, try a neck strap, either worn around your neck or wound around your wrist. It keeps the camera handy and makes you less likely to drop it. Eveready cases enclose the camera and have a front that folds down for picture taking. They provide protection but can be tedious to take off and put on. Gadget bags are good for carrying extra items. Lenses can be kept in plastic bags to protect them from dust, with lens caps both back and front for additional protection of lens surfaces. Aluminum cases with fitted foam compartments provide the best protection against jolts and jars; their disadvantage is that they are not conveniently carried on a shoulder strap. In a high-theft area, some photographers prefer a case that doesn't look like a camera case—for example, a sports bag or a small backpack. A beat-up case that looks as though it contains sneakers and a sweatsuit is less likely to be stolen than one that shouts "cameras."

Battery power is essential to the functioning of most cameras. If your viewfinder display begins to fail or act erratically, the batteries may be getting weak. Many cameras have a battery check that will let you test battery strength; it's a good idea to check batteries before beginning a day's shooting or a vacation outing and to carry spares in your camera bag. If you don't have spares and the batteries fail, try cleaning the ends of the batteries and the battery contacts in the camera with a pencil eraser or cloth; the problem may just be poor contact. Warming the batteries might also bring them back to life temporarily.

Cameras and film in transit should be protected from excessive heat; for example, avoid putting them in a glove compartment on a hot day. Excessive heat not only affects the quality of film, it can soften oil in the pores of metal in the camera, causing the oil to run out and create mischief such as jamming lens diaphragm blades. At very low temperatures, meter batteries and other mechanisms may be sluggish, so on a cold day it is a good idea to carry the camera under your coat until you're ready to take a picture. On the beach, protection from salt spray and sand is vital. Accidental immersion in salt water can occur, however; it is best treated by an immediate and thorough rinse in fresh water, slow drying in a slightly warmed environment (like a gas oven with only the pilot on), followed by a trip to the repair shop as soon as possible. Your only consolation will be that you are not the first one to have this happen.

If a camera will not be used for a while, release the shutter, turn off the exposure meter, and store the camera away from excessive heat, humidity, and dust. Operate the shutter occasionally, because it may become balky if not used. For long-term storage, remove batteries, since they can corrode and leak.

Protecting a camera from dust and dirt is the primary purpose of ordinary camera care. Load and unload film or change lenses in a dust-free place if you possibly can. When changing film, blow or brush around the camera's film-winding mechanism and along the film path. This will remove dust as well as tiny bits of film that can break off and work into the camera's mechanisms. Be careful of the shutter curtain when doing this; it is delicate and should be touched only with extreme care. You may want to blow occasional dust off the focusing mirror or screen, but a competent camera technician should do any work beyond this. Never lubricate any part of the camera yourself.

The lens surface must be clean for best performance, but keeping dirt off of it in the first place is much better than too-frequent cleaning, which can damage the delicate lens coating. Particularly avoid touching the lens surface with your fingers, because they can leave oily prints that may corrode the coating. Keep a lens cap on the front of the lens when it is not in use and on the back of the lens as well if the lens is removed from the camera. During use, a lens hood helps protect the lens surface in addition to shielding the lens from stray light.

To clean the lens you will need a soft rubber squeeze bulb, like an ear syringe, a soft brush, lens tissue, and lens cleaning fluid. Avoid cleaning products made for eyeglasses; they are too harsh for lens surfaces. Shirttails, a clean handkerchief, or paper tissues are usable in an emergency, but lens tissue is much better. ∎

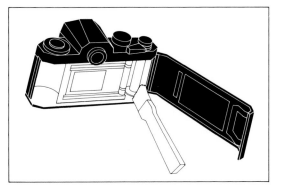

Cleaning inside the camera When you blow or dust inside the camera, tip the camera so the dust falls out and isn't pushed farther into the mechanism. Do not touch the delicate shutter curtain unless absolutely necessary.

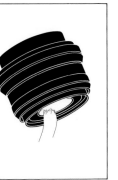

Cleaning the lens First, blow or brush any visible dust off the lens surface. Holding the lens upside down helps the dust fall off the surface instead of just circulating on it.

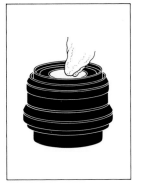

Using lens cleaning fluid Dampen a wadded piece of tissue with the fluid and gently wipe the lens in a circular direction. Don't put lens fluid directly on the lens since it can run to the edge and soak into the barrel. Finish with a gentle, circular wipe with a dry tissue.

Chapter 2
· THE NIKON LENS ·

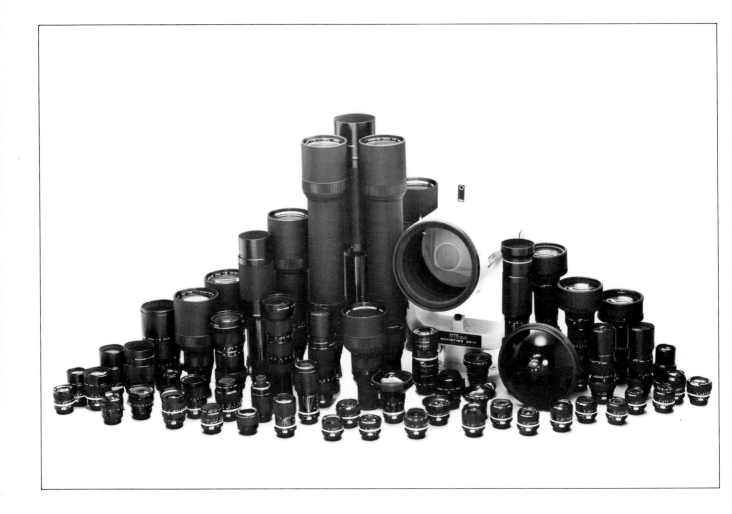

Forming an image Although a good lens is essential for making crisp, sharp photographs, you don't actually need one to take pictures. A primitive camera can be constructed from little more than a shoebox with a small pinhole at one end and a piece of film at the other. A pinhole won't do as well as a lens, but it does form an image of objects in front of it.

A simple lens, as in a magnifying glass, will also form an image—one that is brighter and sharper than an image formed by a pinhole. But a simple lens has many optical defects or aberrations that prevent it from forming an image that is sharp and accurate. A modern compound lens eliminates these aberrations by combining several lens elements ground to different thicknesses and curvatures so that in effect they cancel out each other's aberrations.

Lens speed The main function of lenses is to project a sharp image onto the film, but, in addition, lenses vary in design, with different types made to perform some jobs better than others. The two major differences are in speed and focal length. Lens speed is not the same as shutter speed; it is rather the widest aperture to which the lens diaphragm can be opened. A lens that is "faster" than another opens to a wider aperture and admits more light; it can be used in dimmer light or at a faster shutter speed.

Lens focal length An even more important lens characteristic is focal length. One of the advantages of a Nikon camera is the interchangeability of its lenses; the reason photographers own more than one lens is so that they can change lens focal length. More about focal length appears on the following pages. ▪

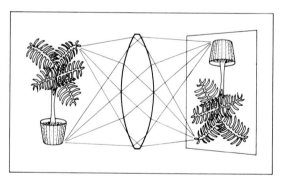

A simple lens forms an image of an object, but because of inherent defects or aberrations in this type of lens, the image is subject to various distortions and is not very sharp.

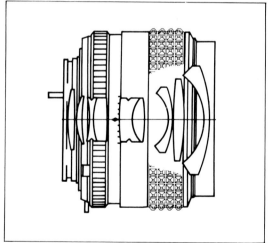

A modern compound lens combines several lenses ground to different specifications that largely cancel out each other's defects. In recent years Nikon designers, aided by computers, have produced a great variety of new lenses with improved image sharpness and lens speed.

LENS FOCAL LENGTH: THE BASIC DIFFERENCE BETWEEN LENSES

Photographers generally describe lenses in terms of their focal length; they refer to a normal, long, or short lens, a 100mm lens, a 35–70mm zoom lens, and so on. Focal length affects the image formed on the film in two important and related ways: the amount of the scene shown (the angle of view) and thus the size of objects (their magnification).

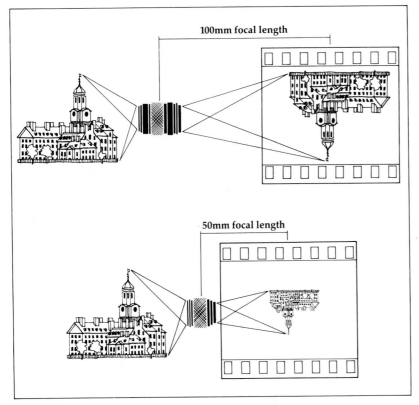

100mm focal length

50mm focal length

Focal length is measured from the optical center of a lens to the image it forms on the film. It is measured when the lens is sharply focused on an object in the far distance (technically known as infinity). Magnification, the size of an object in an image, is one important characteristic that is affected by focal length. As the focal length increases, the size of the object increases. A 100mm lens produces an image twice as large as one produced by a 50mm lens.

How focal length affects an image

The shorter the focal length of a lens, the more of a scene the lens takes in and the smaller it makes each object in the scene appear in the image. You can demonstrate this by looking through a circle formed by your thumb and forefinger. The shorter the distance between your hand (the lens) and your eye (the film), the more of the scene you will see (the greater the angle of view), and since more objects will be shown on the same size negative, the smaller all of them will have to be (the less the magnification). This is similar to the difference between filling a negative with an image of one person's head or with a group of twenty people. In the group portrait, each person's head is smaller.

Interchangeable lenses are convenient. The amount of the scene shown and the size of objects can also be changed by moving the camera closer to or farther from the subject, but the additional option of changing lens focal length gives you much more flexibility and control. Sometimes it is impossible to get closer to your subject—for example, if you are standing on shore photographing a boat on a lake. Sometimes it is difficult to get far enough away, as when you are photographing a large group of people in a small room.

With a single-lens-reflex you can remove one lens and put on another when you want to change focal length. Interchangeable lenses range from super-wide-angle fisheye lenses to extra-long telephotos. A zoom lens is a single lens with adjustable focal lengths. ■

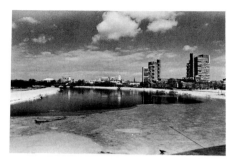

18mm

100°

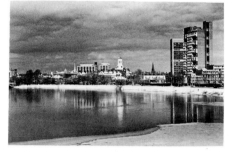

35mm

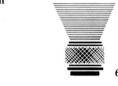

62°

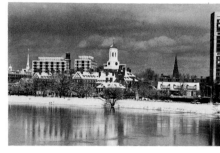

50mm

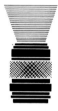

46°

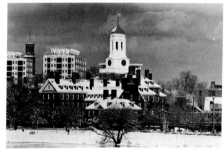

85mm

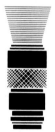

28.5°

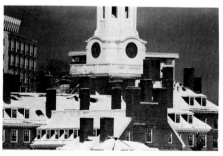

200mm

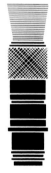

12.5°

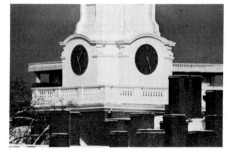

1000mm
focal length

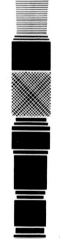

2.5° angle of view

What happens when you change lens focal length? With a given size of film, the amount of a scene included in the image (angle of view) and the size of objects (magnification) are changed if the focal length of the lens is changed. To make this sequence, the photographer changed only the focal length of the lenses, while the distance from lens to subject remained the same. As the focal length increased, for example, from 18mm to 35mm, the angle of view narrowed and the size of objects increased.

NORMAL FOCAL LENGTH: THE MOST LIKE HUMAN VISION

In photography, as in most things, *normal* implies that something is similar to the way most people do or see things. A lens of normal focal length, as you might expect, produces an image on film that seems normal when compared with human vision. The image includes about the same angle of view as the human eye sees clearly, and the relative size and spacing of near and far objects appear normal. For 35mm cameras, this effect is produced by a lens of about 50mm focal length, and 35mm cameras typically are fitted by manufacturers with lenses of this type. The size of the film used in a particular camera determines what focal length is normal for that camera; cameras that use film sizes larger than 35mm have proportionately longer focal lengths for their normal lenses.

Normal lenses have many advantages. Compared with those of shorter or longer focal length, normal lenses are generally faster: they can be designed with wider maximum apertures to admit the maximum amount of light.

Therefore, they are the most suitable lenses for low light levels, especially where action is involved, as in theater or indoor sports scenes or in low light levels outdoors. They are a good choice if the camera is to be hand held since a wide maximum aperture permits a shutter speed fast enough to eliminate lens movement during exposure. Generally, the normal lens is more compact and lighter in weight, as well as somewhat less expensive, than comparable lenses of longer or shorter focal length.

Normal focal length can vary. The "normal" focal length used by a particular photographer—the focal length lens usually fitted on his or her camera—is a matter of personal preference. Many photographers use a lens with a focal length of 35mm as their normal lens because they like its wider view and greater depth of field. Some use an 85mm lens because they prefer its narrower view, which can concentrate the image on the central objects of interest in the scene. ▪

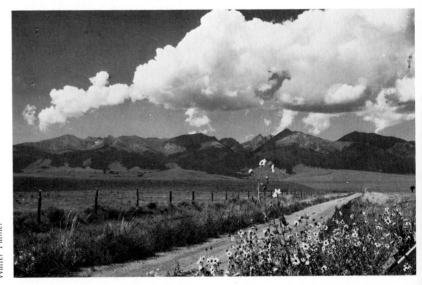

Walter Palmer

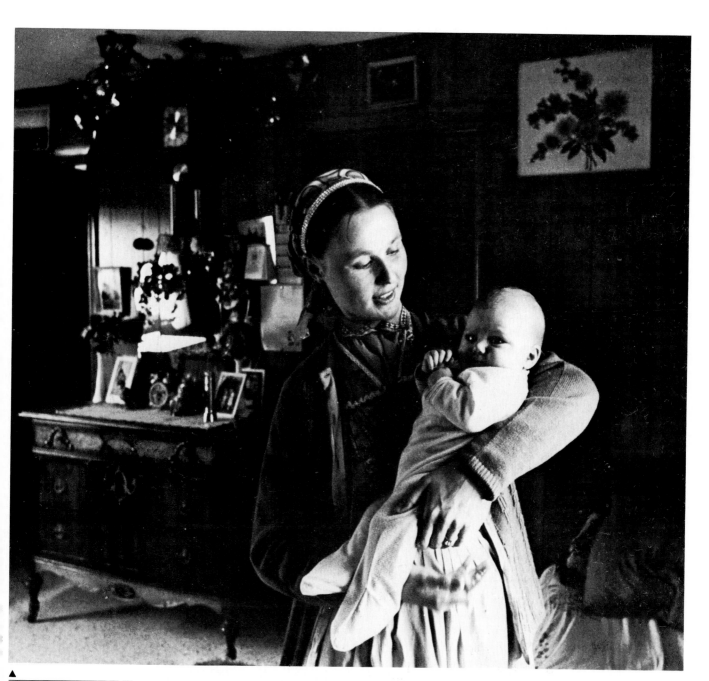

▲
A lens of normal focal length produces an image that appears similar to that of normal human vision. The amount of the scene included in the image and the relative size and placement of near and far objects are what you would expect to see if you were standing by the camera. The scene does not appear exaggerated in depth, as it might with a short-focal-length lens, nor do the objects seem compressed and too close together, as sometimes happens with a long-focal-length lens.

LONG FOCAL LENGTH: TELEPHOTO LENSES

A lens of long focal length seems to bring things closer, just as a telescope does. As the focal length gets longer, less of the scene is shown (the angle of view narrows), but what is shown is enlarged (the magnification increases). This is useful when you are so far from the subject that a lens of normal focal length produces an image that is too small. Sometimes you can't get really close—at a sports event, for example; sometimes it is better to stay at a distance, as in nature photography. An intercepted pass, the President descending from Air Force One, and an erupting volcano are all possible subjects for which you might want a long lens.

A long lens has relatively little depth of field. When you use long lenses, you'll also notice that as the focal length increases, depth of field decreases so that less of the scene is in focus at any given f-stop. For example, a 200mm lens at f/8 has less depth of field than a 100mm lens at f/8. Sometimes this is inconvenient—for example, if you want objects in the foreground of a scene as well as those in the background to be sharp. But it can also work to your advantage by permitting you to eliminate unimportant details or a busy background by photographing them out of focus.

A long lens can seem to compress space. Though traffic was heavy in New York on the day this picture was taken, the long-focal-length lens used by the photographer made the scene look even more crowded than it was. When do you get this effect, and why? See pages 34–35 to find out.

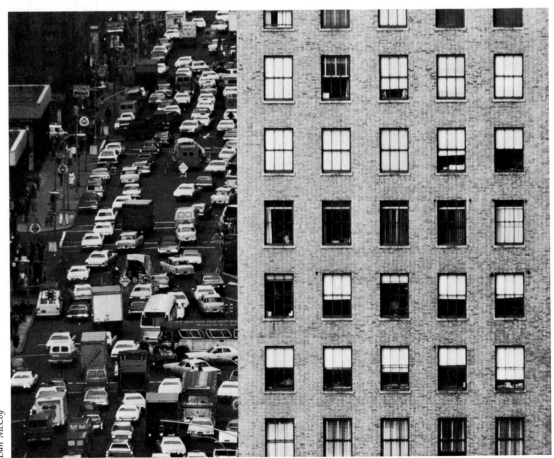

Dan McCoy

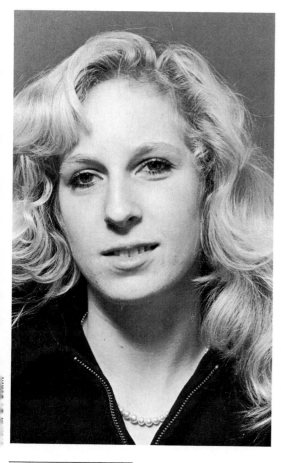

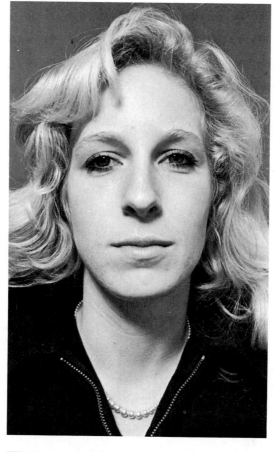

Portrait with a medium-long lens A medium-long lens of 85–135 mm is particularly useful for portraits because the photographer can be relatively far from the subject and still fill the image frame. Many people feel more at ease when photographed if the camera is not too close, and a moderate distance between camera and subject eliminates the distortion of perspective that occurs when a lens is used very close. A good working distance would be 6–8 ft. (2–2.5 m).

Portrait with shorter lens To get a head-and-shoulders image of the same subject with a lens of normal focal length (50 mm), the photographer had to move in close. Photographing a person from very close makes the size of the features nearest to the camera unnaturally large and sometimes even grotesque. If this same lens were used farther back, the subject's head would be small, perhaps too small to enlarge to the desired size without loss of quality.

A long lens, compared with one of normal focal length, is larger, heavier, and somewhat more expensive. Its largest aperture is relatively small; f/4 or f/5.6 is not uncommon. It must be focused carefully because with its shallow depth of field there will be a distinct difference between objects that are sharply focused and those that are not. A faster shutter speed is needed to hand hold because the enlarged image magnifies even a slight movement of the lens during exposure. These disadvantages increase as the focal length increases, but so do the long lens's unique image-forming characteristics. ■

SHORT FOCAL LENGTH: WIDE-ANGLE LENSES

Lenses of short focal length are also called wide-angle or wide-field lenses, which describes their most important feature—they view a wider angle of a scene than human vision does. A lens of normal focal length records what you see when you look at a scene with eyes fixed in one position. A wide-angle lens is like sweeping your vision from side to side, from your left shoulder to your right shoulder for the 180° viewing angle of a 7.5 fisheye lens or slightly from side to side for the 63° angle of a lens of 35mm focal length.

A short lens has great depth of field. The shorter the focal length of a lens, the more of a scene that will be sharp (if the f-stop and distance from the subject remain unchanged). A 28mm lens stopped down to f/8 can be sharp from less than 6.5 ft. (2 m) to infinity (as far as the eye or lens can see), which often will eliminate the need for focusing once the lens has been preset for maximum depth of field.

Wide-angle "distortion" A wide-angle lens can seem to distort an image and produce strange perspective effects. Sometimes these effects are actually caused by the lens, as with a fisheye lens (page 29). But, more often, what seems to be distortion in an image made with a wide-angle lens is caused by the photographer shooting very close to the subject, which is easy to do with this type of lens. A 28mm lens, for example, will focus as close as 1 ft. (0.3 m), and shorter lenses even closer. Any object seen from close up appears larger than an object of the same size that is at a distance. While you are at a scene, your brain knows if you are very close to an object and ordinarily you would not even notice any visual exaggeration. In a photograph, however, you notice size comparisons immediately. See photographs at right. •

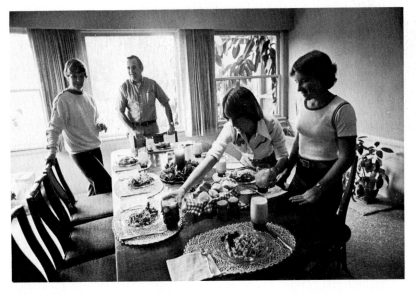

Short lenses are popular with photojournalists, feature photographers, and others who shoot in fast-moving and sometimes crowded situations. For example, many photojournalists use 35mm or 28mm lenses instead of 50mm (normal-focal-length) lenses. These medium-short lenses give a wider angle of view than a 50mm lens, which makes it easier to photograph in close quarters (as in this family dining room). Medium-short lenses also have more depth of field, which can let a photographer focus the lens approximately, instead of having to fine-focus every shot.

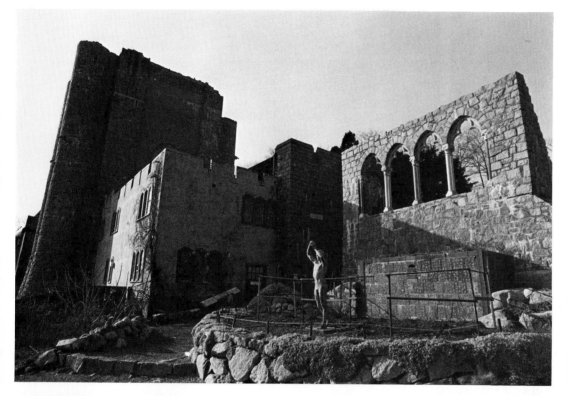

Short lenses show a wide view. Short-focal-length lenses are useful for including a wide view of an area. They have great depth of field so that objects both close to the lens and far from it will be in focus, even at a relatively large aperture.

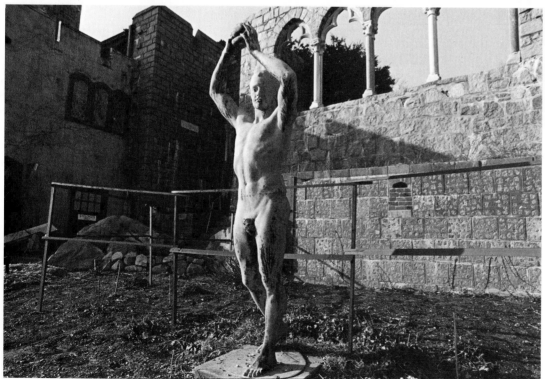

Objects up close appear larger. A short lens can produce strange perspective effects. Since it can be focused at very close range, it can make objects in the foreground large in relation to those in the background. With the lens close to the statue, it looks larger relative to the buildings behind it than it does in the photograph above.

ZOOM, MACRO, AND FISHEYE LENSES

In addition to the usual range of short-, normal-, and long-focal-length lenses, there are other lenses that can view a scene in a new way or solve certain problems with ease.

Zoom lenses combine a range of focal lengths into one lens (see below). The glass elements of the lens can be moved in relation to each other; thus infinitely variable focal lengths are available within the limits of the zooming range. Using a 50–135mm zoom, for example, is like having a 50mm, 85mm, and 135mm lens instantly available, plus any focal length in between. Though zoom lenses are relatively high-priced and somewhat bulky and heavy, one of them will replace two or more fixed-focal-length lenses. Zoom lenses are best used where light is ample since they have a relatively small maximum aperture. New designs give considerably improved sharpness compared

with earlier zoom lenses, which were significantly less sharp than fixed-focal-length lenses.

Macro lenses are used for close-up photography (opposite, top). Their optical design corrects for the focusing faults that can occur at very short focusing distances, but they can also be used at normal distances. Their main disadvantage is relatively small maximum aperture, often about f/3.5 for a 50mm lens. (More about close-up photography in Chapter 5.)

Fisheye lenses have a very wide angle of view—up to 180°—and they exaggerate to an extreme degree differences in size between objects that are close to the camera and those that are farther away (opposite, bottom). They actually distort the image by bending straight lines at the edges of the picture. ▪

A zoom lens gives you a choice of different focal lengths within the same lens. The rectangles overlaid on the picture show some of the ways you could have made this photograph by zooming in to shoot at a long focal length or zooming back to shoot at a shorter one.

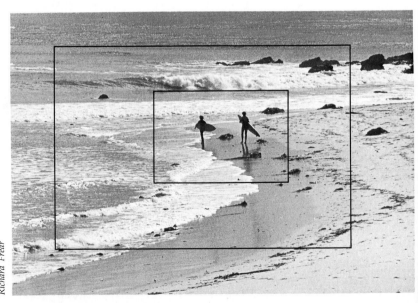

Richard Frear

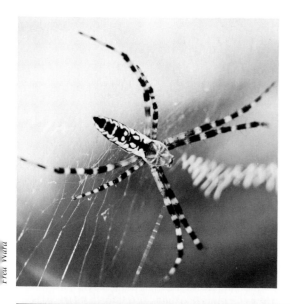

A macro lens enabled the photographer to move in very close to this denizen of the Florida Everglades without having to use supplemental close-up attachments such as extension tubes.

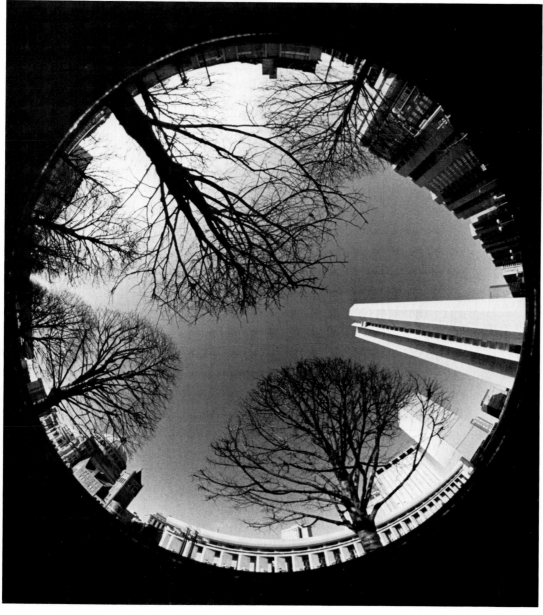

A fisheye lens bent the buildings in this city scene into a round globe shape. Objects at the edge of the fisheye's image circle are distorted more than they are toward the center.

DEPTH OF FIELD: SHARPNESS IN A PHOTOGRAPH

Depth of field Dead sharp from foreground to background, totally out of focus except for a narrow strip, or sharp to any extent in between—it is possible to choose how sharp your image will be. When you focus a camera on an object, the distance between lens and film is adjusted by turning the lens barrel until the object is sharp on the viewing screen. In most cases

The depth of field, the area in a scene that is acceptably sharp, extended in the top picture on this page from the flowers in the foreground to the greenhouse windows in the background. For another picture (bottom) the photographer wanted only part of the scene to be sharp. See opposite for ways to control the depth of field in a photograph.

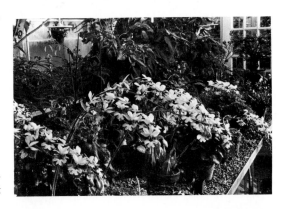

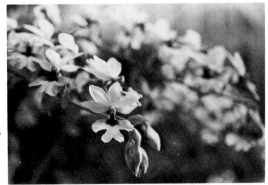

Alan Oransky

part of the scene will be acceptably sharp both in front of and behind the most sharply focused plane. Objects will gradually become more and more out of focus the farther they are from the sharply focused area. This depth within which objects appear acceptably sharp in the image—the depth of field—can to a certain extent be increased or decreased.

Controlling the depth of field When you make a picture you can manipulate three things that affect the depth of field (illustrations opposite). Notice that changing the depth of field may at the same time change the image in other ways.

Aperture size Stopping down the lens to a smaller aperture, for example, from f/2 to f/16, increases the depth of field. As the aperture gets smaller, more of the scene will be sharp in the print.

Focal length Using a shorter-focal-length lens also increases the depth of field at any given f-number. For example, more of a scene will be sharp when photographed with a 50mm lens at f/8 than with a 200mm lens at f/8.

Lens-to-subject distance Moving farther away from the subject increases the depth of field most of all, and simply stepping back with your camera will make more of a scene sharp in the print. This is particularly true if you start out very close to the subject. ▪

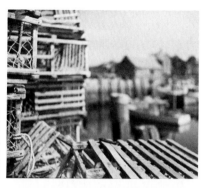

Fredrik D. Bodin

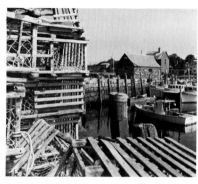

The smaller the aperture (with a given lens), the greater the depth of field. Using a smaller aperture for the picture on the right made the image much sharper. With the smaller aperture, the amount of light reaching the film decreased, so a slower shutter speed had to be used to keep the total exposure the same.

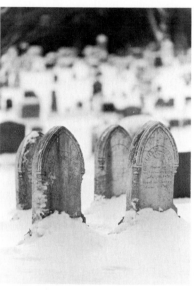

Fredrik D. Bodin

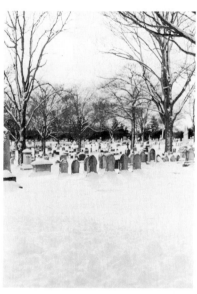

The shorter the focal length of the lens, the greater the depth of field. Notice that changing to a shorter focal length for the picture on the right also changed the angle of view (the amount of the scene shown) and the magnification of objects in the scene.

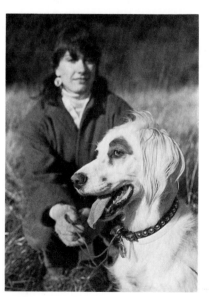

Fredrik D. Bodin

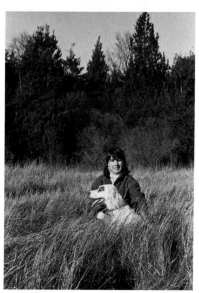

The farther you are from a subject, the greater the depth of field. The photographer stepped back to take the picture on the right. If you focus on an object far enough away, the lens will form a sharp image of all objects from that point out to infinity.

31

MORE ABOUT DEPTH OF FIELD: HOW TO PREVIEW IT

When photographing a scene, you will often want to know the extent of the depth of field—how much of the scene will be sharp. You may want to be sure that certain objects are sharp. Or you may deliberately want something out of focus, such as a distracting background. To control what is sharp, you need some way of gauging the depth of field.

With zone focusing you can be ready for an action shot by focusing in advance, if you know approximately where the action will take place. Suppose you are on a ski slope and you want to photograph a skier coming down the hill. The nearest point at which you might want to take the picture is 15 ft. (4.5 m) from the action; the farthest is 30 ft. (9 m).

Line up the distance scale so that these two distances are opposite a pair of f-stop indicators on the depth-of-field scale (with the lens shown at right, below the two distances fall opposite the f/16 indicators). Now, if your aperture is set to f/16 or smaller, everything from 15–30 ft. (4.5–9 m) will be within the depth of field and in focus.

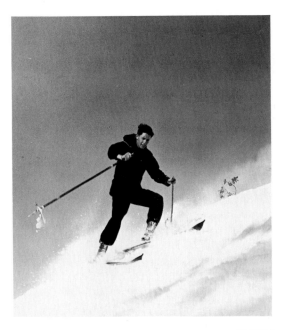

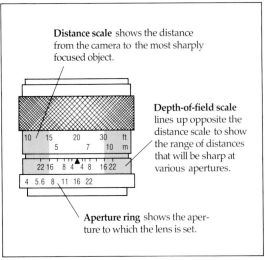

Distance scale shows the distance from the camera to the most sharply focused object.

Depth-of-field scale lines up opposite the distance scale to show the range of distances that will be sharp at various apertures.

Aperture ring shows the aperture to which the lens is set.

Checking the depth of field   For viewing, the lens aperture is ordinarily wide open, and the viewing screen shows the scene with the depth of field at its shallowest. When the shutter release is pressed, the lens automatically stops down to the taking aperture and the depth of field increases. Some cameras have a previewing mechanism so that, if you wish, you can stop down the lens to view the scene at the taking aperture and see how much will be sharp.

However, if the lens is set to a very small aperture, the stopped-down image on the screen may be too dark to be seen clearly. If so, the nearest and farthest limits of the depth of field can be read on the depth-of-field scale on the lens barrel (this page, bottom). Manufacturers also prepare printed tables showing the depth of field for different lenses at various focusing distances and f-stops.

Zone focusing for action   Knowing the depth of field in advance is useful when you want to preset the lens to be ready for an action shot without last-minute focusing. Zone focusing uses the depth-of-field scale on the lens to set the focus and aperture so that the action will be photographed well within the depth of field (this page, top).

Focusing for the greatest depth of field   When you are shooting a scene that includes important objects at a long distance as well as some that are closer, you will want maximum depth of field. Shown opposite is a way of setting the lens to permit as much as possible of the scene to be sharp. ∎

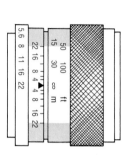

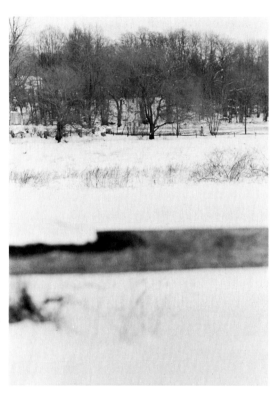

When the lens is focused on infinity (∞ on the lens distance scale), everything at that point or farther away will be sharp: with this lens at f/22 everything will be sharp from 50 ft. (16 m) to infinity (as far as the eye can see). In the picture at left everything is sharp from the bushes in the pasture to the farthest point in the background.

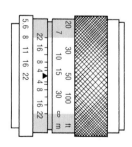

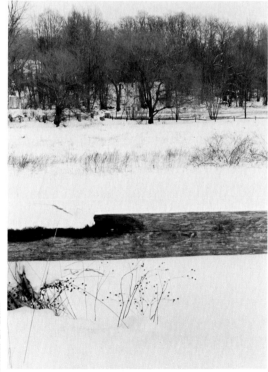

Fredrik D. Bodin

You can increase the depth of field even more if, instead of focusing on infinity, you set the infinity mark (∞) opposite the point on the depth-of-field scale that shows the f-stop you are using. You are now focused on a distance (50 ft., 16 m.) slightly closer than infinity (technically called the hyperfocal distance). Now everything from the plank of the fence in the foreground (25 ft., 8 m) to the far background is within the depth of field and will be sharp in the print.

PERSPECTIVE: HOW A PHOTOGRAPH SHOWS DEPTH

Perspective: the impression of depth Few lenses (except for the fisheye) actually distort reality. The perspective in a photograph—the apparent size and shape of objects and the impression of depth—is what you would see if you were standing at camera position. Why then do some photographs seem to have an exaggerated depth, with the subject appearing stretched and expanded (this page, top), while other photographs seem to show a compressed space, with objects crowded very close together (this page, bottom)? The brain judges depth in a photograph mostly by comparing objects in the foreground with those in the background, and the greater the size differences

Expanded perspective A short-focal-length lens used close to a subject stretches distances because it magnifies objects near the lens in relation to those that are far from the lens.

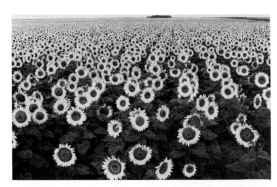

Compressed perspective A long-focal-length lens used far from a subject compresses space. Size differences and the impression of depth are minimized because the lens is relatively far from both foreground and background.

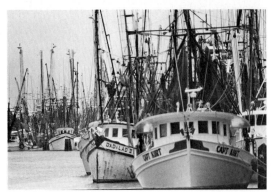

Fredrik D. Bodin

perceived, the greater the impression of depth. When viewing an actual scene, the brain has other clues to the actual distances, and it disregards any apparent distortion in sizes. But when looking at a photograph, the brain uses relative sizes as the major clue.

How perspective is controlled in a photograph Any lens moved in very close to the foreground of a scene increases the impression of depth by increasing the size of foreground objects relative to objects in the background. As shown opposite, perspective is not affected by changing the focal length of the lens if the camera remains at the same distance. However, it does change if the distance from lens to subject is changed.

Perspective can be exaggerated. Perspective effects are exaggerated when changes occur in both focal length and lens-to-subject distance. A short-focal-length lens used close to the subject increases differences in size because it is much closer to foreground objects than to those in the background. This increases the impression of depth. Distances are magnified and sizes and shapes may be distorted when scenes are photographed in this way.

The opposite effect occurs with a long-focal-length lens used far from the subject. Differences in sizes are decreased because the lens is relatively far from *all* objects. This decreases the apparent depth and sometimes seems to squeeze objects into a smaller space than they could occupy in reality. ▪

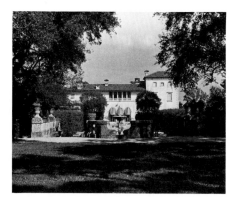 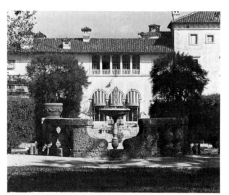 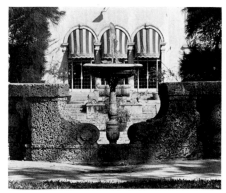

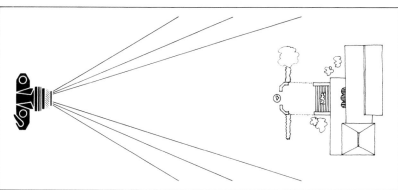

Alan Oransky

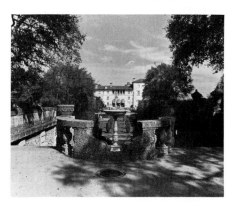

Changing focal length alone does not change perspective—the apparent size or shape of objects or their apparent position in depth. As the focal length was increased for the photographs above, the size of all the objects increased at the same rate. Thus, the impression of depth remained the same.

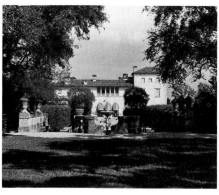 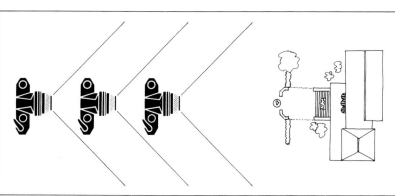 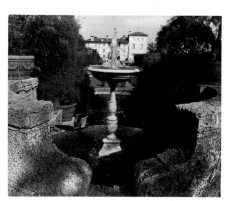

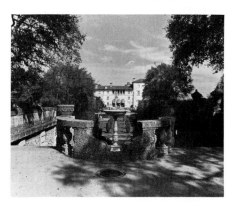

Lens-to-subject distance controls perspective. Perspective is changed when the distance from the lens to objects in the scene is changed. Here, though the focal length remained the same, the impression of depth increased as the camera was brought closer to the subject.

LENS PERFORMANCE: GETTING THE MOST FROM A LENS

Lens motion causes blur. Though some photographers claim to be able to hand hold their cameras steadily at slow shutter speeds—1/15 sec. or even slower—it takes only a slight amount of lens motion during exposure to cause a noticeable blur in an image. If a sharp picture is your aim, using a fast shutter speed or supporting the camera on a tripod is a much safer bet for producing an image that will be sharp when enlarged.

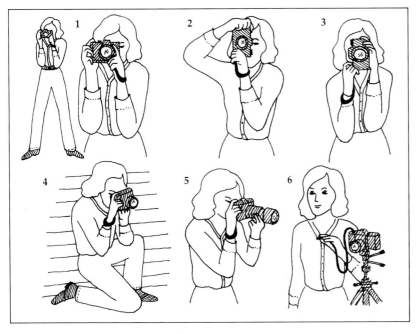

Preventing blur due to lens motion
The focal length of the lens you are using determines how fast a shutter speed you need to keep an image acceptably sharp during a hand-held exposure. The longer the focal length, the faster the shutter speed must be, because a long lens magnifies any motion of the lens during the exposure just as it magnifies the size of the objects photographed. As a general rule, the slowest shutter speed that is safe to hand hold can be matched to the focal length of the lens. That is, a 50mm lens should be hand held at a shutter speed of 1/50 sec. or faster, a 100mm lens at 1/100 sec. or faster, and so on. This doesn't mean that the camera can be freely moved during the exposure. At these speeds the camera can be hand held, but with care. At the moment of exposure, hold your breath and squeeze the shutter release smoothly.

A tripod will help you in situations that require a slower shutter speed than is feasible for hand holding, for example, at dusk when the light is dim. A tripod is also useful when you want to compose a picture carefully or do close-up work. It is standard equipment for copy work, such as photographing another photograph or something from a book, because hand holding at even a fast shutter speed will not give the critical sharpness that resolves fine details to the maximum degree possible. A cable release also helps by triggering the shutter without your having to touch the camera directly, so the camera stays absolutely still.

1. To hand hold a camera steadily, keep feet apart and rest the camera lightly against your face. Hold your breath and squeeze the shutter release gently.
2. With the camera in a vertical position, the left hand focuses and holds the camera with the left elbow against the chest. The right arm is raised to release the shutter.

3. In this vertical position, the right hand holds the camera and releases the shutter; the left hand focuses and helps steady the camera.
4. In kneeling position, kneel on one leg and rest your upper arm on the other knee. Leaning against a wall or a steady object will help brace your body.

5. With a long lens on the camera, use one hand to support the weight of the lens. Winding the camera strap around your wrist helps to steady the camera and to prevent dropping it.
6. A tripod and cable release provide the steadiest support and are essential for slow shutter speeds if a sharp image is desired.

Stray light can cause problems. You can't make an exposure without light, but light can also be the undoing of your picture. The sun, a bright bulb, or other light source within the image can cause ghosting, bright spots in the shape of the lens diaphragm that show in the picture. The spots are caused by stray light bouncing around inside the lens.

Flare, an overall graying of the image, is also caused by stray light. Though the sun itself was not in the picture below left, sunlight struck the lens at an angle. The result was an additional exposure of non-image-forming light that reduced picture contrast.

A lens hood helps. Flare is best controlled by using a lens hood or shade to shield the lens from direct light. Lens hoods come in different sizes and should be matched to the focal length of your lens. Too small a hood can cut into the image and vignette the edges (below, right). Check the viewfinder image carefully for vignetting if you are using a filter plus a lens hood or two filters together. ▪

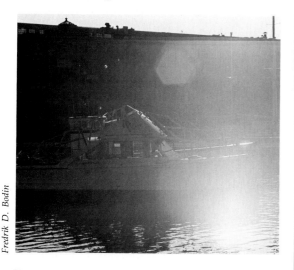

Fredrik D. Bodin

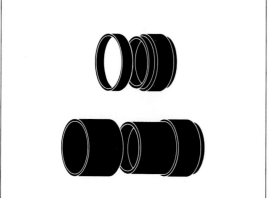

◀**Lens hoods** clip or screw onto the front of a lens and are made in different sizes to match different focal lengths.

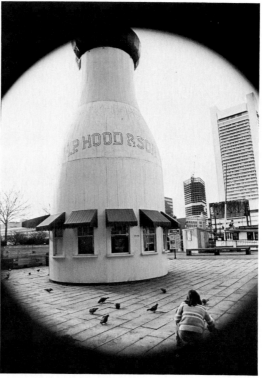

Fredrik D. Bodin

◀**Light problems** Flare (far left) grays the image when light strikes the front of the lens, even if the light source is not in the picture. Vignetting (left) is the result of using a lens hood that is too small and so cuts into the image area.

Chapter 3
· FILM AND EXPOSURE ·

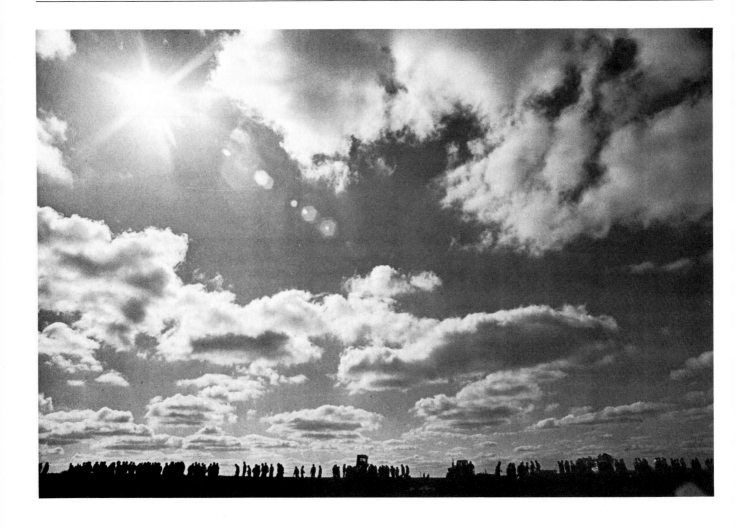

The exposure of film to light is one area in which a little expertise pays off in much better pictures. Exposing the film correctly (that is, setting the shutter speed and aperture so they let in the correct amount of light for a given film and scene) makes the difference between a rich image with realistic tones, dark but detailed shadows, and bright, delicate highlights and a too dark, murky picture or a picture that is barely visible because it is too light.

At the simplest level, you can rely on the chart of exposure recommendations the film manufacturer provides with each roll of film. You can also let an exposure meter or automatic exposure system make decisions for you.

In many cases these standardized procedures will give you a satisfactory exposure. But standard procedures don't work in all situations. If the light source is behind the subject, for example, an average reading will silhouette the subject against the brighter background. This may not be what you want.

You will have more control over your pictures—and be happier with the results—if you know how to interpret the information the meter provides and how to adjust the recommended exposure to give any variation you may choose. You will be able to select what you want to do in a specific situation rather than exposing at random and hoping for the best. ▪

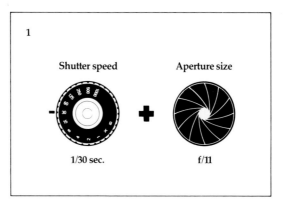

Shutter speed   Aperture size

1/30 sec.   f/11

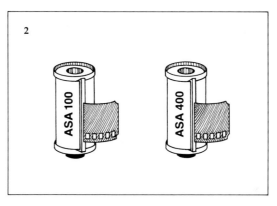

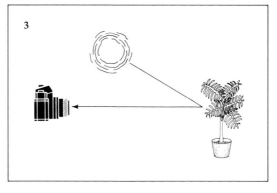

Learning to expose film properly is not hard. To let just the right amount of light into the camera, you need to understand just three things:

1. How the shutter speed and the size of the lens opening (the aperture) work together to control light (pages 10–15).

2. The sensitivity of each kind of film to light—the film's speed (pages 42–43).

3. How to meter the light to measure its brightness and then set the exposure, either automatically or manually (pages 50–55).

FILM CHARACTERISTICS: HOW FILM WORKS

The light sensitivity of film The most basic characteristic of film is that it is light-sensitive; it undergoes a chemical change when exposed to light. Light is energy, a visible form of the wavelike energy that extends in a continuum from radio waves through visible light to gamma rays. These forms of energy differ only in their wavelengths, the distance from the crest of one wave to the crest of the next. The visible part of this spectrum, the light that we see, ranges between 400 and 700 nanometers, or billionths of a meter.

Not all films respond the same way to light. Silver halides, the light-sensitive part of film, respond primarily to blue and ultraviolet wavelengths, but dyes can be incorporated in the emulsion to increase their range of sensitivity. General-purpose black-and-white and color films are panchromatic, or pan; they are designed to be sensitive to most wavelengths of the visible spectrum so that the image they record is similar to that perceived by the human eye. Some special-purpose films are designed to be sensitive to other parts of the spectrum. Orthochromatic (or ortho) black-and-white films are sensitive primarily to blue and green wavelengths. Infrared films are sensitive to infrared wavelengths that are invisible to the eye (see page 46). Since some films are designed to perform certain jobs better than others, it is useful to be aware of their characteristics. ▪

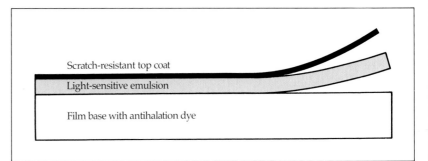

Film cross section
Film is made up of layers of different materials. On top is a tough coating that helps protect the film from scratches during ordinary handling. Next is a layer of gelatin emulsion that contains the light-sensitive part of the film, silver halide crystals. (Color film has several layers of halides, each sensitive to a different part of the spectrum.) An adhesive bonds the emulsion to the base, a flexible support of either cellulose acetate or polyester. To prevent light rays from bouncing back through the film to add unwanted exposure to the emulsion, an antihalation dye that absorbs light is added to the film base.

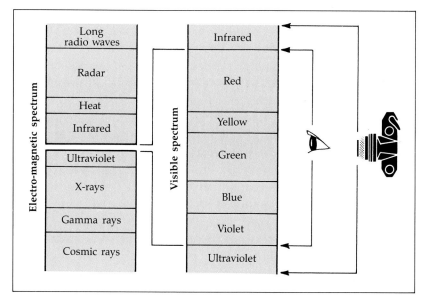

Electro-magnetic spectrum	Visible spectrum
Long radio waves	Infrared
Radar	Red
Heat	Yellow
Infrared	Green
Ultraviolet	Blue
X-rays	Violet
Gamma rays	Ultraviolet
Cosmic rays	

Light   When certain wavelengths of energy strike the human eye, they are perceived as light. Film is manufactured so that it too is sensitive to this part of the electromagnetic energy spectrum. In addition, film is sensitive and responds to certain wavelengths that the eye cannot see, such as ultraviolet and infrared light.

Film terms

Color sensitivity   The parts of the visible spectrum to which a film responds. See above.

Film speed   The overall sensitivity of a film to light as compared with other films. See next page.

Latitude   The degree to which film can be overexposed or underexposed and still produce an acceptable print or slide.

Grain   The granularity or speckled effect produced by tiny specks of silver in the emulsion clumping together. See next page.

Contrast   The range of tones from dark to light that a film produces. Films of normal contrast show blacks, whites, and a wide range of tones in between. High-contrast black-and-white films record all the tones in a scene as either black or white or something close to these extremes.

Emulsion   The light-sensitive coating applied to photographic films and papers. It consists of silver halide crystals of silver

chloride, silver bromide, and silver iodide, plus other chemicals, suspended in gelatin. The ability of silver halides to darken on exposure to light makes photography possible.

Base   The backing of film or paper on which emulsion is coated.

Negative   An image, usually on film, with tones that are the opposite of those in the original scene; light areas in the original are dark in the negative, dark areas are light.

Positive   An image on paper or film with tones that are the same as those in the original scene.

Transparency   Usually, a positive color image on film. A slide is a transparency mounted in a small frame of cardboard or other material so it can be inserted in a projector or viewer.

Reversal processing   The procedure by which a positive image is made directly from a scene or from another positive; making a color slide directly from film exposed in the camera is an example.

FILM SPEED AND GRAIN: THE TWO GO TOGETHER

Film speed ratings How sensitive a film is to light, that is, how much it darkens when exposed to a given quantity of light, is indicated by its film speed number (in English-speaking countries, an ISO or ASA rating). The more sensitive—or faster—the film, the higher its number in the rating system. (See box opposite: Film speed ratings.)

A high film speed is often useful: the faster the film, the less exposure it needs to produce an image, and so fast films are often used for photographing in dim light. But along with fast film speed go some other characteristics: an increase in grain and decrease in contrast and often in sharpness. As the illustrations on this page show, the most detailed image was produced by the slow, ASA 32 film. The very fast ASA 2475 film, by comparison, gave a mottled, grainy effect and recorded less detail.

Graininess occurs when the bits of silver that form the image clump together. It is more likely to occur with fast films, which have large silver halide crystals, than it is with slower films having smaller crystals. The effect is more noticeable in big enlargements or if the film is not processed at consistent temperatures, if it is overexposed, or if it is "pushed" to increase its film speed by special development.

What film speed should you use? Theoretically, for maximum sharpness you should choose the slowest film usable in a given situation. For practical purposes, however, many photographers use a medium-fast (ASA 100–200) film in most situations and switch to a slow film only when extremely fine detail is of special importance. ▪

Film speed and grain Generally speaking, the slower the film (the lower the ASA, DIN, or ISO number), the finer the grain structure of the film and the more detailed the image the film records. Compare these extreme enlargements. Film speed also affects the color qualities of color materials like slide films.

ASA 32

ASA 400

ASA 2475

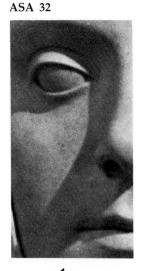
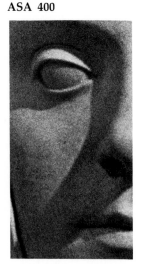
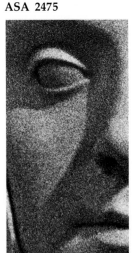

Alan Oransky

Slower film speed ← ── Less grain ── More detail ── More contrast

Film speed ratings

Film speeds are given in one of three rating systems: ASA, DIN, or ISO. Film manufacturers are now standardizing film speed listings, using the ISO system, which may in time simplify things. Don't be overly concerned about the numerical soup; the first thing to remember is simply that the higher the number in a given rating system, the faster the film, that is, the less light it will need for a correct exposure.

An ASA (American Standards Association) rating is found on films sold in English-speaking countries. Each time the ASA number doubles, the film speed doubles. ASA 200 is twice as fast as ASA 100, half as fast as ASA 400.

A DIN (Deutsche Industrie Norm) rating is common in European countries. Each time the rating increases by 3, the film speed doubles. DIN 24 (equivalent to ASA 200) is twice as fast as DIN 21, half as fast as DIN 27.

The ISO (International Standards Association) system is becoming the universal rating system for film speed listings, but ISO-rated films may still vary somewhat in the way they are listed. A film with a speed equivalent to ASA 200 (DIN 24) may be listed as ISO 200/24 (combining the ASA and DIN numbers), ISO/ASA 200, or simply ISO 200.

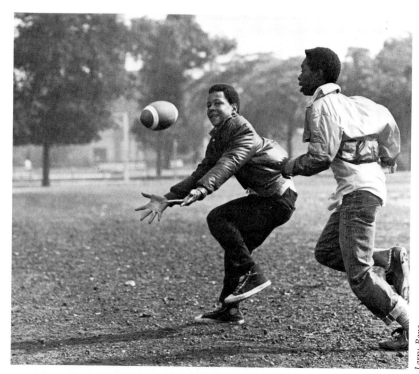

Larry Rana

▲
A fast film, ASA 400, let the photographer use a shutter speed of 1/500 sec., fast enough to guarantee that action would be sharp in the picture and fast enough to let him shoot freely, hand holding the camera, without fear that camera motion would blur the picture overall. A fast film is particularly important indoors or when light is dim, but was useful even in this scene outdoors.

A slow film, ASA 32, ▶ recorded fine detail and texture in this forest scene. The image would be crisp and detailed even if enlarged to a much bigger size than shown here.

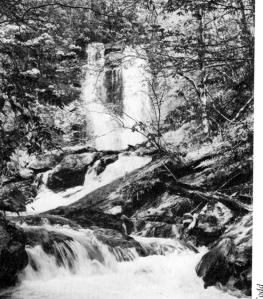

Daniel O. Todd

BUYING AND USING FILM

Buying film Whatever kind of film you buy, check the expiration date printed on the film package before you make your purchase. The film will still be usable beyond that date but it will steadily deteriorate.

Storing film Heat accelerates the deterioration of film, so avoid storing it in warm places like the inside of a glove compartment on a hot day or the top of a radiator on a cold one. Room temperature is fine for short-term storage, but for longer storage a refrigerator or freezer is better. Be sure that the film to be chilled is in a moisture-proof wrapping, and when you remove the film from refrigeration, avoid condensation of moisture on the film surface by letting it come to room temperature before opening.

Airport security X-ray devices are supposed to be safe for film. However, they can cause fogging of either unexposed or exposed but undeveloped film if the machines are not adjusted correctly or if the same film is subjected to repeated doses, for example, on a trip that involves several flights. Lead-lined film bags are available that give protection from X-rays. Or you can simply ask to have film (and camera, if it is loaded) inspected by hand to reduce the possibility of X-ray damage.

Loading Light exposes film, and you want only the light that comes through the lens to strike the film. So, load and unload your camera away from strong light to avoid the possibility of stray light leaking into film cassettes and causing streaks of unwanted exposure. Outdoors, at least block direct sun by shading the camera with your body when loading it. ▪

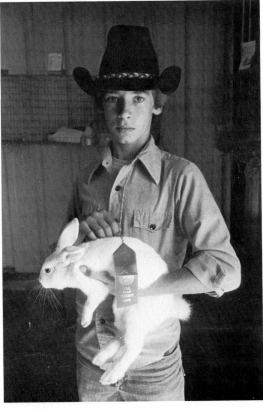

John Running

A fast film, such as one rated at ASA 400 or 1000, is good not only for action shots but for any situation in which the light is relatively dim and you want to work with a fast shutter speed or a small aperture.

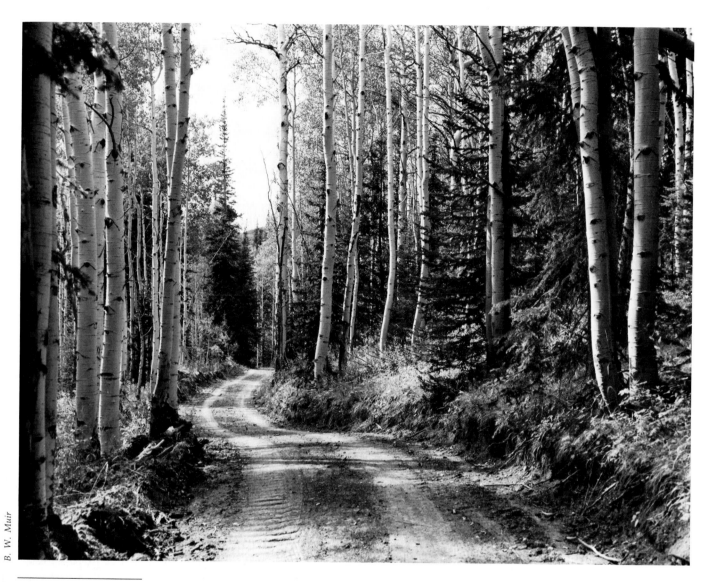

B. W. Muir

A medium-speed film, ASA 125, was chosen for this photograph of a forest road. The fine grain and excellent sharpness of the film recorded every detail of the delicate shading on the tree trunks and intricate pattern of leaves.

SPECIAL-PURPOSE FILMS:
HIGH-CONTRAST AND INFRARED

Most films are designed to "see" as the human eye does and to respond to light in ways that appear realistic. But some films depart from the reality that we know.

High-contrast black-and-white film does not record a continuous range of tones from black through many shades of gray to white; instead it translates each tone in a scene into either black or white (see illustration below). Some 35mm materials are specially made for high-contrast photography. Some continuous-tone films (like Panatomic X) can also be specially processed for high contrast.

Infrared black-and-white film is sensitized to wavelengths that are invisible to the human eye, the infrared waves that lie between visible red light and wavelengths that produce heat. Since the film responds to light that is not visible to the eye, it can be used to photograph in the dark. The sun is a strong source of infrared radiation, and tungsten filament lamps, flash bulbs, and electronic flash can also be used. Unusual and strangely beautiful images are possible because many materials reflect and absorb infrared radiation differently from visible light (see opposite). Grass, leaves, and other vegetation reflect infrared wavelengths very strongly and thus appear very bright, even white. Clouds too are highly reflective of infrared wavelengths, but since the blue sky does not reflect them, it appears dark, even black, in a print.

Because the wavelengths are invisible, you cannot fully visualize in advance just what the print will look like—sometimes a frustration, but sometimes an unexpected pleasure. The correct exposure is also something of a guess; most meters do not measure infrared light accurately. (See box opposite: Using infrared film.) Infrared color film is also available. ▪

High-contrast film changes the many shades of gray in an ordinary scene into a graphic abstraction of blacks and whites.

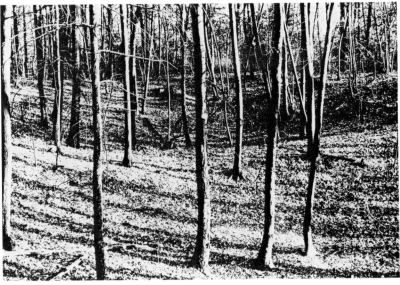

Stanley Rowin

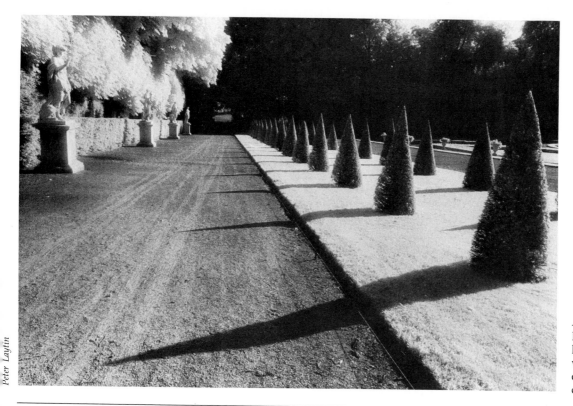

Peter Laytin

Infrared film records leaves and grass as very light. The result can be a strangely dreamlike landscape.

Using infrared film

Storage and loading Infrared film can be fogged by exposure to heat or even slight exposure to infrared radiation. Do not buy infrared film that is not refrigerated, and once you have it, store it under refrigeration when possible. Load and unload the camera in total darkness, either in a darkroom or with the camera in a changing bag.

Focusing Most lenses focus infrared wavelengths slightly differently from the way they focus visible light. With black-and-white infrared film, after focusing as usual, rack the lens forward very slightly as if you were focusing on an object closer to you. Some lenses have a red indexing mark on the lens barrel to show the adjustment needed. The difference is very slight, so unless depth of field is very shallow (as when you are photographing close up), you can usually make do without any correction. No correction is needed for infrared color film.

Filtration See manufacturer's instructions. Kodak recommends a No. 25 red filter for general use with black-and-white infrared film to enhance the infrared effect by absorbing the blue light to which the film is also sensitive. Kodak recommends a No. 12 minus-blue filter for general use with color infrared film.

Exposure A general-purpose exposure meter, whether built into a camera or hand-held, cannot reliably measure infrared radiation. Kodak recommends the following manually set trial exposures for its films. High-Speed Infrared black-and-white film used with No. 25 filter: distant scenes—1/125 sec. at f/11; nearby scenes—1/30 sec. at f/11. Ektachrome Infrared color film with a No. 12 filter: 1/125 sec. at f/16. After making the trial exposure, make additional exposures of 1/2 stop and 1 stop more and 1/2 stop and 1 stop less (see Bracketing, page 49).

NORMAL, UNDER-,
AND OVEREXPOSURE

A negative is the first image that is produced when film is exposed to light. A negative is the reverse of the original scene: the brightest areas in the scene are the darkest in the negative. How does this happen? When light strikes film, the energy of the light activates light-sensitive silver halide crystals in the film emulsion. The energy rearranges the structure of the crystals so that during development they convert to particles of dark metallic silver.

The more light that strikes a particular area, the more the light-sensitive crystals are activated, and the darker that part of the negative will be. As a result, a white canoe, for example, will be very dark in the negative. If film is exposed to light long enough, it darkens simply by the action of light, but ordinarily it is exposed only long enough to produce a latent or invisible image that is then made visible by chemical development.

To get a positive print from the negative, the negative is printed, usually by shining light through it, on a piece of light-sensitive paper. Where the original scene was bright (the white canoes), the negative is very dark and dense with many particles of silver. Dense areas in the negative block light from the positive; few particles of silver form there, and the areas are bright in the final image.

The opposite happens with dark areas like the darker parts of the water in the original scene: dark areas reflect little light, so only a little silver (or sometimes, none) is produced in the negative. When the positive is made, these thin or clear areas in the negative pass much light to the positive and form dark deposits of silver corresponding to the dark areas in the original scene. When a positive transparency like a color slide is made, the negative is chemically processed into a positive.

Exposure determines the darkness of the image. The exposure you give a negative (the combination of f-stop and shutter speed) determines how much light reaches the film and how dark the negative will be: the more light, the darker the negative, and, in general, the lighter the final image. The correct exposure for a given situation depends on how you want the photograph to look.

Film and paper have exposure latitude, that is, a good print can often be made from a less-than-perfect negative. Color slides have the least latitude: for best results they should not be overexposed or underexposed more than ½ stop (1 stop is acceptable for some scenes). See page 63 for more about exposing color film. Black-and-white or color prints can be made from negatives that vary somewhat more: from about 1 stop underexposure to 2 stops overexposure is usually acceptable.

But with too much variation from the correct exposure, prints and slides begin to look bad. Too much light overexposes the negative; it will be much too dense with silver to pass enough light to the final print, which in turn will be too pale (illustrations, opposite bottom). Conversely, too little exposure produces a negative that is too thin, resulting in a print that is much too dark (illustrations, opposite top).

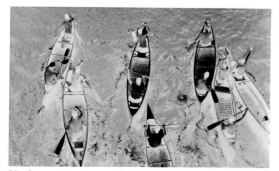

Underexposed negative

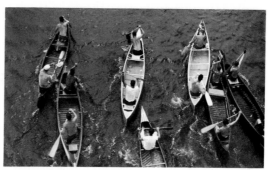

Dark positive

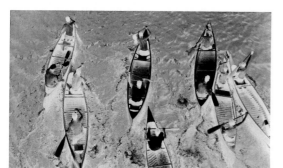

Normal negative

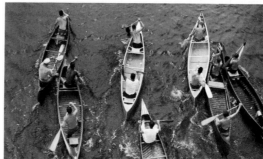

Normal positive

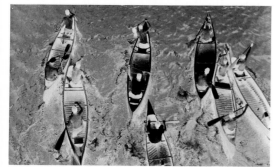

Overexposed negative

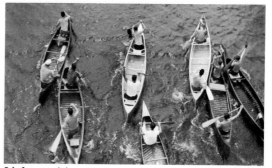

Light positive

B. W. Muir

Bracketing helps if you are not sure about the exposure. To bracket, you take several photographs of the same scene at different exposure settings. First make an exposure with the aperture and shutter speed set by the automatic system or manually set at the combination you think is the right one. Then make a second shot with 1 stop more exposure, and a third shot with 1 stop less exposure. This is easy to do if you are setting the exposure manually: for 1 stop more exposure, either set the shutter to the next slower speed or the aperture to the next larger opening (the next smaller f-number); for 1 stop less exposure, either set the shutter to the next faster speed or the aperture to the next smaller opening (the next larger

f-number). Usually, one of the three shots will be about right.

How do you bracket with automatic exposure? That depends on your camera. Some models have an exposure compensation dial with which you can set in a fixed amount of exposure change. Other cameras have a back-light button, which when depressed gives an additional 1 or 1½ stops of exposure. Even if your camera has neither of these features and only functions automatically, so you cannot set the exposure manually, you can still bracket by adjusting the film speed dial: for 1 stop additional exposure, divide the film speed in half and reset the film speed dial accordingly; for 1 stop less exposure, multiply the film speed by 2 and reset the dial. ∎

EXPOSURE METERS: WHAT DIFFERENT TYPES DO

Exposure meters vary in design but they all perform the same basic function. They measure the brightness of light, then, for a given film speed, they calculate f-stop and shutter speed combinations that will produce a properly exposed negative.

Meters built into cameras The light-sensitive part of a camera meter is a photoelectric cell. When the metering system is turned on and the lens of the camera pointed at a subject, the cell measures the brightness of that subject. To use that reading to expose the picture with automatic exposure operation, you set either the aperture or the shutter speed and the camera adjusts the other to let in the correct amount of light. Some cameras may set both shutter speed and aperture. With manual exposure operation, you adjust the aperture and shutter speed based on the viewfinder readout.

Hand-held meters When the cell of a hand-held meter (one that is not built into a camera) is exposed to light it moves a needle across a scale of numbers or activates a digital display. The greater the amount of light, the higher the reading. When the arrow on the calculator dial is set opposite the same number that appears on the needle scale, a series of recommended f-stop and shutter speed combinations are lined up. See illustration below.

Meter batteries Some hand-held meters and all meters built into cameras are powered by small batteries. It is important to check the batteries regularly (see manufacturer's instructions for how to do this). An exhausted battery will cause the meter to give the wrong reading or to cease functioning altogether. ▪

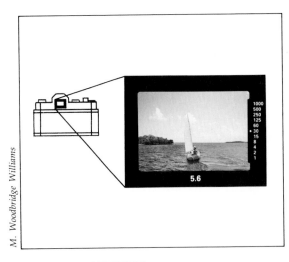

M. Woodbridge Williams

A through-the-lens (TTL) meter, built into the camera, is a key feature of SLR cameras. The viewfinder shows the area that the meter is reading. A TTL meter may be coupled to the camera to set the exposure automatically or it may simply indicate the correct exposure to set.

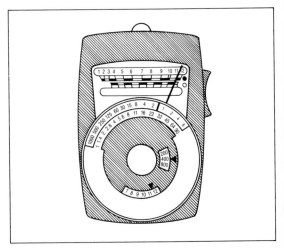

A hand-held meter is separate from the camera. After measuring the brightness of a subject, the meter's calculator dial or other readout shows recommended f-stop and shutter speed combinations for correct exposure.

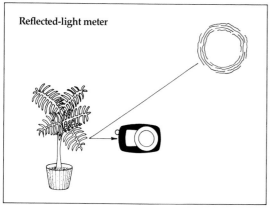

Reflected-light meter

◀ **A reflected-light meter** measures the amount of light reflected from an object. To make a reading, point the meter at the entire scene or at a specific part of it. Most hand-held meters and all of those built into cameras are reflected-light meters.

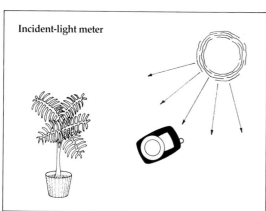

Incident-light meter

◀ **An incident-light meter** measures the amount of light falling on an object. The meter's light-sensitive cell is pointed at the camera to measure the amount of light falling on the subject as seen from camera position.

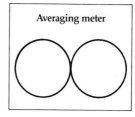

Averaging meter

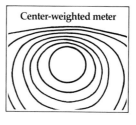

Center-weighted meter

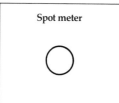

Spot meter

How much of a scene does a reflected-light meter measure? An averaging or overall meter reads most of the image area and computes an exposure that is the average of all the brightnesses in the scene. Center-weighted meters overlap their readings to concentrate on the central area of an image, which is usually the important one to meter. A spot meter reads only a small part of the image. Very accurate exposures can be calculated with a spot meter, but it is important to select with care the area to be read.

Aperture-priority exposure The photographer chooses the aperture, and the camera mechanism adjusts the shutter speed.

Aperture-priority automatic exposure

You set aperture	f/2		f/2.8	f/4	f/5.6	f/8
Shutter speed then adjusts	1/250 sec.		1/125	1/60	1/30	1/15

Cameras with automatic exposure have shutter speed and aperture controls connected to the meter.

Shutter-priority exposure The photographer sets the shutter speed, and the camera mechanism changes the aperture until the correct exposure is set.

Shutter-priority automatic exposure

You set shutter speed	1/250 sec.	1/125	1/60	1/30	1/15
Aperture then adjusts	f/2	f/2.8	f/4	f/5.6	f/8

Programmed exposure The camera sets both shutter speed and aperture.

Programmed automatic exposure

Camera sets shutter speed	1/250 sec.	1/125	1/60	1/30	1/15
Camera sets aperture	f/2	f/2.8	f/4	f/5.6	f/8

MAKING AN EXPOSURE
OF AN AVERAGE SCENE

A single-lens-reflex camera with a built-in meter, and especially a camera with automatic exposure control, makes photography enjoyable and easy. With automatic operation, you simply point the camera at your subject, focus, and shoot. In most cases, the meter and its accompanying automatic circuitry let just the right amount of light in to expose the scene correctly.

A reflected-light meter averages the light entering its angle of view. These meters, whether built into the camera or hand held, are calibrated on the assumption that in an average scene all the tones—dark, medium, and light—will add up to an average medium gray. So the meter and its accompanying circuitry sets, or recommends, an exposure that will record all of the light it is reading as medium gray in the photograph.

This works well if you are photographing an "average" scene, one that has an average distribution of light and dark areas, and if the scene is evenly illuminated as viewed from camera position, that is, when the light is coming more or less from behind you or when the light is evenly diffused over the entire scene (see illustrations this page). The illustrations on the facing page show you how to meter this type of average or low-contrast scene.

A meter can be fooled, however, if your subject is surrounded by a much lighter area such as a bright sky or by a much darker area such as a large dark shadow. See pages 54–55 for what to do in such cases. ∎

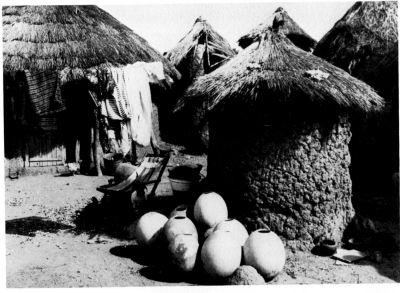

A. Defever

▲
An overall meter reading works well when a directly lit scene is evenly illuminated as seen from camera position. When light is shining directly on a subject, even illumination occurs when the main source of light—here, the sun—is more or less behind you as you face the subject. Shadows are dark but do not obscure important parts of the scene.

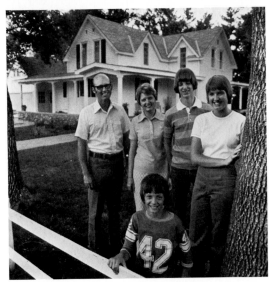

◄**A scene in diffused light also photographs well with an overall reading,** for example, outdoors in the shade or on an overcast day or indoors when the light is coming from several light sources. Diffused light is indirect and soft. Shadows are not as dark as they would be in direct light, so all parts of the scene are clearly visible.

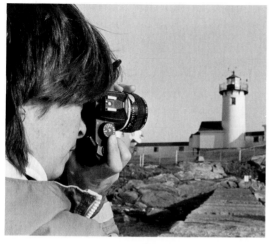

Using a meter built into a camera

1. Set the film speed into the camera.

2. Select the exposure mode: automatic (aperture-priority, shutter-priority, or programmed, if you have a choice) or manual.

3. As you look through the viewfinder at the subject, activate the meter to read the brightness of the scene.

4a. In aperture-priority mode, select an aperture that gives the desired depth of field. The camera will select a shutter speed; make sure that it is fast enough to prevent blurring of the image caused by camera or subject motion.

4b. In shutter-priority mode, select a shutter speed fast enough to prevent blur. The camera will select an aperture; make sure

that it gives the desired depth of field.

4c. In programmed mode, the camera will select both aperture and shutter speed for you.

4d. In manual mode, you set both aperture and shutter speed based on the readout shown in the camera's viewfinder.

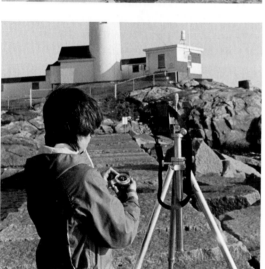

Calculating exposure with a hand-held, reflected-light meter

1. Set the film speed into the meter.

2. Point the meter's photoelectric cell at the subject at the same angle seen by the camera. Activate the meter to measure

the brightness of the light reflected by the subject.

3. Line up the number registered by the indicator needle with the arrow on the meter's calculator dial.

4. Choose one of the combinations of f-stops and shutter

speeds shown on the calculator dial and set the camera accordingly. Any combination shown on the dial lets the same quantity of light into the camera and produces the same exposure.

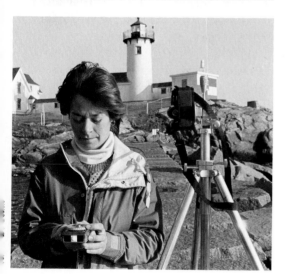

Calculating exposure with an incident-light meter

1. Set the film speed into the meter.

2. Point the meter's photoelectric cell away from the subject—toward the camera lens. Activate the meter to measure the brightness of the light fall-

ing on the subject. (Make sure that the same light that is falling on the subject is falling on the meter. For example, take care not to shade the meter if the subject is brightly lit.)

Proceed as in steps 3 and 4 for reflected-light meter.

EXPOSING SCENES WITH HIGH CONTRAST

"It came out too dark." Sometimes even experienced photographers complain that they metered a scene carefully but the picture still wasn't properly exposed. All an exposure meter or an automatic exposure system can do is measure light. It can't think or reason, so it doesn't know what part of a scene you are interested in or whether a particular object is supposed to be light or dark. You have to think for the meter and sometimes change the exposure it recommends, especially with a scene of high contrast, in which the light areas are much brighter than the dark areas.

What types of scenes cause exposure problems? The most common is a subject against a much brighter background, such as a sunny sky (see illustration below). Because the meter averages all the tonal values—light, medium and dark—in the scene, it assumes that the entire scene is very bright. It consequently sets an exposure that lets in less light, which makes the entire picture darker and your main subject too dark. Less common, but occasionally encountered, is a subject against a very large, much darker background. The meter assumes that the entire scene is very dark, so it lets in more light, which makes the main subject too light.

To expose a contrasty scene correctly you will need to measure the light level for the most important part of the picture. There are several ways to do this. First try to meter just the main subject. If you are photographing a person or some other subject against a much darker or lighter background, move in close enough so that you exclude the background from the reading—though not so close that you meter your own shadow. If your main subject is a landscape or other scene that includes a very bright sky, tilt the camera or meter down slightly so you exclude most of the sky from the reading.

A substitution reading is possible if you can't move in close enough to the important part of a contrasty scene. Look for an object of about the same tone in a similar light that you can read instead. For very exact exposures, professional photographers may meter

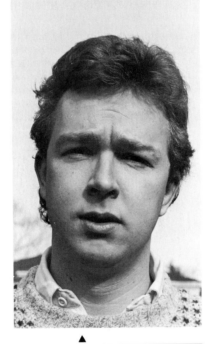

Fredrik D. Bodin

An underexposed (too dark) photograph can result when the light is coming from behind the subject or when the subject is against a very bright background such as the sky. The problem is that a meter aver- ages all the tonal values that strike its light-sensitive cell. Here the photographer pointed the meter so it included the much brighter tone of the sky as well as the person.

▲ **A better exposure for contrasty scenes** results from moving up close to meter only the main subject, as shown above. This way, you take your meter reading from the most important part of the scene.

the light reflected from a gray card, a card of standard middle gray of 18 percent reflectance (meters are designed to calculate exposures for ideal subjects of 18 percent reflectance). You can also meter the light reflected by the palm of your hand (see opposite).

How do you set your camera once you have metered a high-contrast scene? If your camera has a manual exposure mode, just set the shutter speed and aperture to expose the main subject correctly, using the settings from a reading made up close or from a substitution reading. In automatic operation, you will need to override the automatic circuitry to change the exposure. Don't be afraid to do this; only you know the picture you want. All cameras have some means of adjusting the exposure (see page 56). ∎

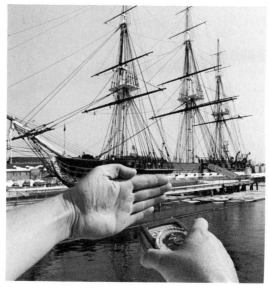

Fredrik D. Bodin

A substitution reading, such as one taken from the palm of your hand, will give you an accurate reading if you can't get close enough to a subject. Try the exposure recommended by the meter if you have very dark skin, but give one stop more exposure if you have light skin, as here.

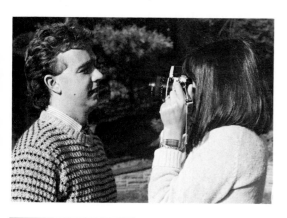

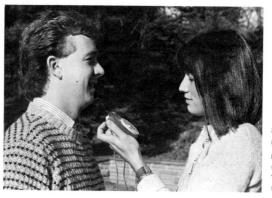

Fredrik D. Bodin

Move in close to meter a high-contrast scene, where the important part of the picture is either much lighter or much darker than other parts of the image.

With a built-in meter, move in (without blocking the light) until the important area just fills the viewfinder. Set the shutter speed and aperture and move back to your original position to take the picture.

With a hand-held, reflected-light meter, move in close enough to read the subject but not so close as to block the light. A spot meter, which reads light from a very narrow angle of view, is particularly useful for metering high-contrast scenes.

CONTROLLING EXPOSURE

All SLR cameras with automatic exposure have some means of overriding the automatic system when you want to increase the exposure to lighten a picture or decrease the exposure to darken it. The change in exposure is measured in "stops." Each aperture setting is one stop from the next setting. Shutter speeds are also described as being one stop apart; each setting is one stop from the next.

Memory lock   An exposure memory switch temporarily locks in an exposure, so you can move up close to take a reading of a particular area, lock in the desired setting, step back, and then photograph the entire scene.

Exposure compensation dial   Moving the dial to +1 or +2 increases the exposure and lightens the picture. Moving the dial to –1 or –2 decreases the exposure and darkens the picture.

Backlight button   If a camera does not have an exposure compensation dial, it may have a backlight button. Depressing the button adds a fixed amount of exposure, 1½ stops, and lightens the picture. It cannot be used to decrease exposure.

Film speed dial   You can increase or decrease exposure by changing the film speed dial. The camera then responds as if the film is slower or faster than it really is. With ASA- or ISO-rated film, doubling the film speed (for example, from ASA 100 to ASA 200) darkens the picture by decreasing the exposure one stop. Halving the film speed (for example, from ASA 400 to ASA 200) lightens the picture by increasing the exposure one stop.

Manual mode   In manual mode, you adjust the shutter speed and aperture yourself. Exposure can be increased to lighten the picture or decreased to darken it, as you wish.

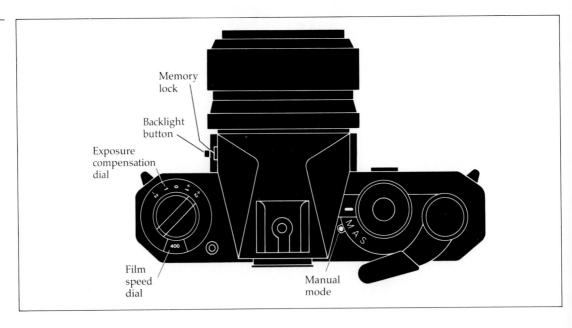

One or more features for controlling exposure are found on all single-lens-reflex cameras.

Memory lock

Backlight button

Exposure compensation dial

Film speed dial

Manual mode

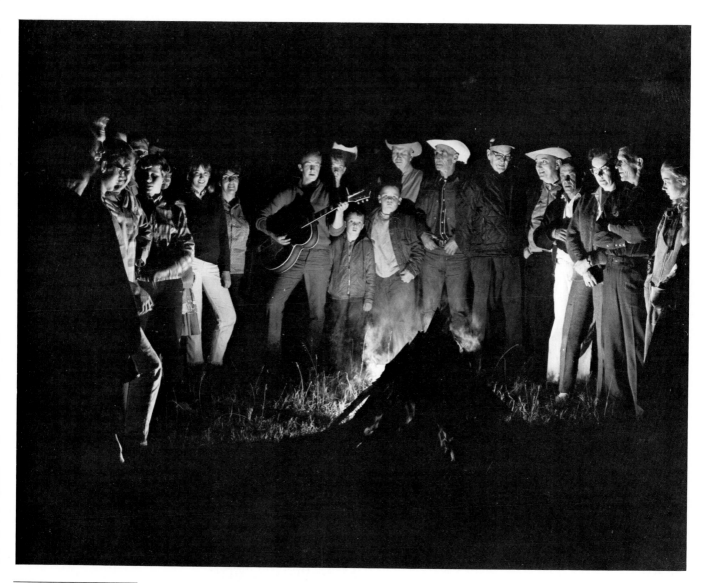

You can use manual mode to set the shutter speed and aperture for photographs at night, like this bonfire scene. More about exposures for unusual lighting situations on the following page.

EXPOSURES IN HARD-TO-METER SITUATIONS

What do you do when you want to make a photograph but can't make a meter reading—photographing fireworks, for instance, or a city skyline at night? Guessing and making a couple of experimental tries is better than nothing, and you might get an image you'll like very much. If you keep a record of the scene and your exposures, you will at least have an idea about how to expose a similar scene.

Bracketing is a good idea: make at least three shots—one at the suggested exposure, a second with 1 or 1½ stops more exposure, and a third with 1 or 1½ stops less exposure. Not only will you probably make one exposure that is acceptable, but each different exposure may be best for a different part of the scene. For instance, at night on downtown city streets a longer exposure may show people best while a shorter exposure will be good for brightly lit shop windows.

In hard-to-meter situations, Kodak suggests the manually set exposures at right for films rated at ASA 400. Give twice as much exposure (1 stop more) for films rated at ASA 125 to ASA 200. Give half as much exposure (1 stop less) for films rated at ASA 1000.

For color pictures of scenes marked with * use a tungsten-balanced film for the most natural color.

You can also use daylight-balanced color film, but your pictures will look yellow-red. For color pictures of scenes marked with † use daylight film. You can also use tungsten film with an 85B (amber) filter over your camera lens; if you do this, give 1 stop more exposure than that indicated in the table. (More about film color balance on pages 64–65.)

	With ASA 400 film
*Home interiors at night—areas with average light	1/30 sec. f/2
*Candlelit close-ups	1/15 sec. f/2
Indoor and outdoor holiday lighting at night, Christmas trees	1/15 sec. f/2
Brightly lit downtown streets	1/60 sec. f/2.8
Brightly lit nightclub or theater districts, e.g., Las Vegas	1/60 sec. f/4
Neon signs and other lit signs	1/125 sec. f/4
Store windows	1/60 sec. f/4
Subjects lit by streetlights	1/15 sec. f/2
Floodlit buildings, fountains	1/15 sec. f/2
Skyline—distant view of lit buildings at night	1 sec. f/2.8
Skyline—10 minutes after sunset	1/60 sec. f/5.6
Fairs, amusements parks	1/30 sec. f/2.8
Amusement park rides—light patterns	1 sec. f/16
Fireworks—displays on ground	1/60 sec. f/4
Fireworks—aerial displays (Keep shutter open for several bursts.)	f/16
Lightning (Keep shutter open for one or two streaks.)	f/11
Burning buildings, campfires, bonfires	1/60 sec. f/4
Subjects by campfires, bonfires	1/30 sec. f/2
*Night football, baseball, race-tracks	1/125 sec. f/2.8
Niagara Falls—white lights Light-colored lights Dark-colored lights	4 sec. f/5.6 8 sec. f/5.6 15 sec. f/5.6
Moonlit—landscapes Snow scenes	8 sec. f/2 4 sec. f/2
*Basketball, hockey, bowling	1/125 sec. f/2
*Boxing, wrestling	1/250 sec. f/2
*Stage shows—average	1/60 sec. f/2.8
*Circuses—floodlit acts	1/60 sec. f/2.8
*Ice shows—floodlit acts	1/125 sec. f/2.8
†Interiors with bright fluorescent light	1/60 sec. f/4
*School—stage and auditorium	1/30 sec. f/2
*Hospital nurseries	1/60 sec. f/2.8
*Church interiors—tungsten light	1/30 sec. f/2

© Eastman Kodak Company, 1978

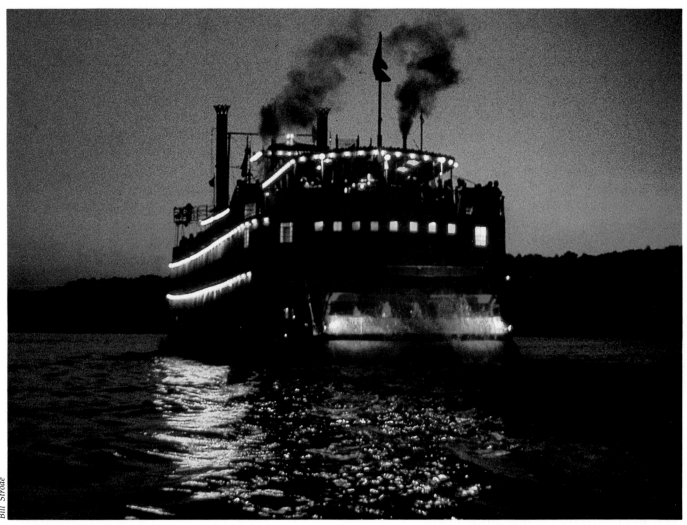

Bill Strode

Very long exposures may turn out too dark even if you think the exposure was calculated correctly. The problem here is that a very long exposure at a very low light level does not affect the film as strongly as you would expect it to (technically this is called the reciprocity effect). For exposures of 1 second or longer, increase the total exposure by ½ to 1 stop; for exposures of 10 seconds or longer, increase 1 to 2 stops; for exposures of 100 seconds or longer, increase 2 to 3 stops. See instructions packed with film for more detailed information. ∎

What exposure would you use with ASA 400 film for this shot at dusk of the riverboat "Belle of Louisville"? If the chart at left doesn't have exactly the situation you are photographing, look for a related one. As a start for an exposure for this scene you might try the one recommended for "Skyline—10 minutes after sunset." Then bracket additional exposures.

Chapter 4
· COLOR ·

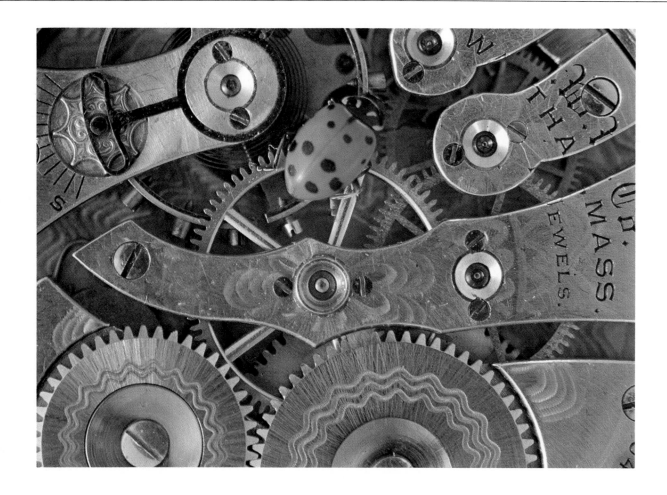

Why a separate chapter on color? The basic camera-handling techniques are the same as for black and white, and you can load a roll of color film, shoot, and probably get pretty good pictures. But you will get more consistent results and be happier with what you get if you know a little about how color film reacts to light. This chapter describes what to expect from color film and how to use it to make better pictures.

Color slides and prints are appealing because color makes a picture seem more realistic than the same scene rendered in black and white. Black-and-white film records the shapes of things and tones from light to dark, but the black-and-white image is still very much an abstraction. An image in color is more like the real one. It is more apt to remind you of exactly how the scene looked when you took the picture and to make viewers who weren't there feel that they are really seeing the scene too.

Color pictures can also be deliberately *un*realistic. A purple sky, a green horse, color streaks, and other manipulations are possible with color materials and may be just what you want on occasion.

Where does color come from? Light from the sun appears to have no tint or color of its own; it is "white" light. But it actually contains all colors, and if you project it through a prism it will separate into a band of colors like a rainbow. A colored object—a leaf, for example—has color because when light strikes it, the leaf reflects the greenish components or wavelengths

of the light while absorbing other colors. The eye is sensitive to these reflected wavelengths and sees them as green. Dyes, in paint or color prints, act just as the leaf does in selectively absorbing and reflecting certain wavelengths of light and so producing color. ▪

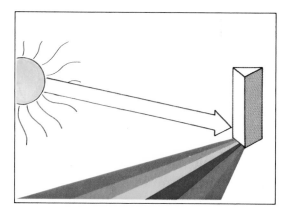

"White" light, such as that from the sun, contains all the colors of the spectrum. Pass light through a prism and it will break into a rainbow of colors.

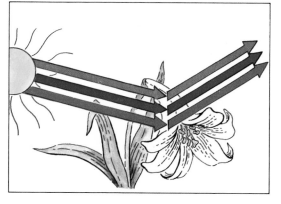

A lily appears white because it reflects all the wavelengths of light that strike it. When these wavelengths reach the eye, the color white is perceived.

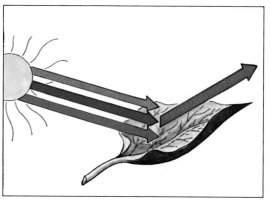

A leaf appears green because when light strikes it, the leaf absorbs all but the wavelengths that create the visual sensation of green.

What can you get in color films?

There are many brands and types of color film on the market. They belong basically to two main categories: negative films and reversal films. A negative film (such as Kodacolor or Agfacolor) produces a negative in which the tones and colors are the opposite of those in the original scene. The negative is then printed on paper or film to make a positive image. A reversal film (such as Kodachrome or Fujichrome) is given special reversal processing to produce a positive transparency or slide.

Color films come in a range of film speeds, from slow (ASA 25) to fast (ASA 1000). Just as with black-and-white films, more film speed brings some increase in grain and decrease in sharpness. Film speed also affects the color rendition of the film, with faster films generally producing less intense colors (less saturation) than slower films. Different films are also made to be used with specific light sources such as sunlight or tungsten light (see pages 64–65).

Negative color film is first processed for a negative image and then the negative is printed to make a positive image. Reversal color film produces the familiar transparency or slide that is viewed by projection; it is a positive color image on the film exposed in the camera. A slide can also be printed on paper, to make another positive image.

Color reversal films vary from brand to brand, and slides of identical film speed from different manufacturers will show variations in color balance, color saturation, grain, and other characteristics. Personal taste is important here, and it is useful to expose the same scene on different types of film and compare the processed slides to choose the film you prefer for future use. Color negative films also vary from brand to brand, but less noticeably than reversal films.

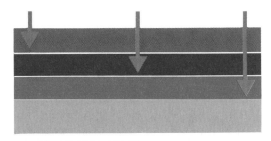

Color film consists of three light-sensitive layers, each of which responds to about one-third of the colors in the light spectrum. Each layer is matched to a primary color dye that is built into the emulsion or added during processing, and every color in the spectrum can be produced by mixing varying proportions of these color primaries.

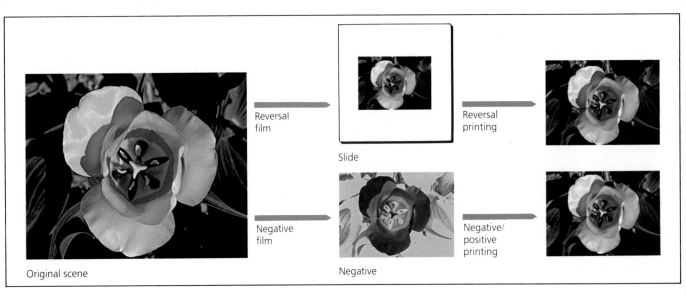

Original scene

Reversal film

Slide

Reversal printing

Negative film

Negative

Negative/positive printing

Correct exposure is essential for slides. If you want slides with clear, brilliant colors and good detail in important parts of the picture, you must expose the film correctly. Too much exposure produces slides that are too light and that have pale, washed-out colors. Too little exposure produces dark, murky slides with little texture or detail. Sometimes you may want to deliberately underexpose or overexpose an image to get these effects, but in most cases, the best results come from exposures that are no more than ½ stop over or under the optimum.

Some scenes are more difficult to expose than others. The easiest scenes to expose correctly are those that are evenly lit, with the meter showing little difference in brightness between the darkest and lightest areas (this page, bottom). Scenes like this can vary as much as 1 stop from the optimum exposure and still produce good results.

If a scene is contrasty, however—if it has dark shadows as well as brilliantly lit areas (this page, top)—often no single exposure will be correct for everything in the scene. If the shadowed areas are exposed correctly, the bright areas will be too light; exposing for the bright areas will make the shadowed ones too dark. Try exposing for the most important area, (pages 54–55), then bracketing additional exposures. Pages 90–91 show you how to brighten shadow areas by adding fill light. Pages 70–71 describe how to use dark shadows for dramatic effect. ▪

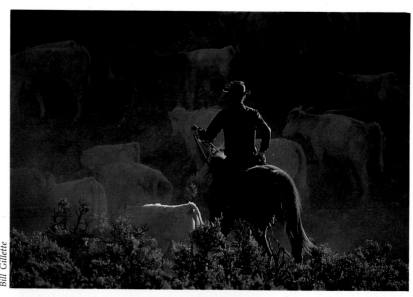

Bill Gillette

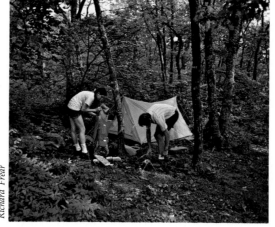

Richard Frear

▲

Backlit scenes and other scenes in bright, direct light often have some important areas very light or others very dark or both. You have to choose which area is the most important to you and meter that part of the scene for your exposure.

Scenes in soft, flat light are the easiest to expose correctly because the lightest areas in the scene are not much brighter than the darkest ones, so there will not be any areas that are too bright or too dark in the final photograph.

COLOR BALANCE:
MATCHING FILM WITH LIGHT SOURCE

The color temperature of light—the mixture of wavelengths of different colors that it contains—varies with different light sources. Daylight, for example, is much bluer than light from an ordinary light bulb. Consequently, different types of color films are balanced to match the color temperatures of specific light sources.

The color temperature of a light source (measured in degrees Kelvin) is a way of describing its color exactly. Color films are made to be used either with daylight, relatively blue in color, or with tungsten light, which is more reddish. The lower the color temperature, the more "warm" red wavelengths there are in the light. Higher color temperatures have more "cool" blue wavelengths.

Film	Color Temperature	Type of Light
	12,000 K and higher	Clear skylight in open shade, snow
	10,000 K	Hazy skylight in open shade
	7000 K	Overcast sky
	6600 K	
	5900-6200 K	Electronic flash
Daylight	5500 K	Midday
	4100 K	
	3750 K	
	3600 K	
	3500 K	
Type A (indoor)	3400 K	Photolamp
Tungsten (indoor)	3200 K	
	3100 K	Sunrise, sunset
	3000 K	
	2900 K	100 watt tungsten bulb
	2800 K	
	1900 K	Candlelight, firelight

Color films are balanced for either daylight or tungsten light. Daylight-balanced films yield the most natural looking colors when shot in daylight or other light that is rich in blue wavelengths. Tungsten-balanced or indoor films produce the best result when used in more reddish light, such as the light from tungsten bulbs. (See illustrations opposite.) Most indoor films are called tungsten-balanced and are designed to be used with light of 3200 K (degrees Kelvin) color temperature; however, they give acceptable results when used with any type of tungsten light. Type A indoor film has a slightly different balance for precise color balance use with high-intensity 3400 K photolamps.

Color balance is important with reversal films. Color slides are made from the film that was in the camera, which should be shot either in the light for which it was intended or with a filter over the lens to adjust the color balance. If this is not done, the resulting slides will have a distinct color cast.

Color temperature is less critical with some films. Color negative films are somewhat tolerant of different color balances because color balance can be adjusted during printing. Some color negative films, such as Kodacolor VR 1000, minimize color balance differences between light sources even more. Black-and-white film can be shot in light of any color temperature. ▪

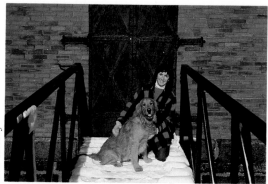

Daylight film in daylight

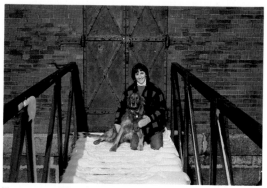

Tungsten film in daylight

Daylight-balanced films are designed for a light source that is rich in blue wavelengths and low in red, such as daylight (especially near noon), electronic flash, and blue flash bulbs (see illustration above left). If you shot the same scene on tungsten-balanced film, the resulting pictures, particularly slides, would look quite blue (see right). Tungsten films can be used in daylight if an 85 (amber) filter is placed over the lens and the exposure increased by about 1 stop.

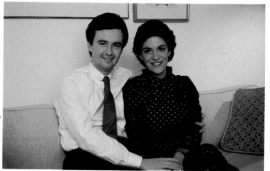

Tungsten film in tungsten light

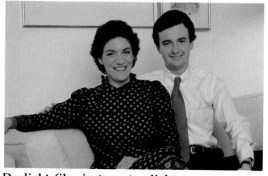

Daylight film in tungsten light

Tungsten-balanced films are designed for a light source that is the opposite of daylight: rich in red wavelengths, low in blue—as from household bulbs, photofloods, and clear flash bulbs (see left). If you shot the same scene on daylight-balanced film, the resulting color balance would be reddish-orange (see right). Daylight film can be corrected for tungsten if an 80 (blue) filter is placed over the lens and the exposure increased by about 2 stops. However, light indoors is often too dim for such an increase.

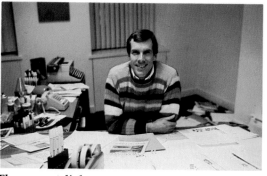

Fluorescent light

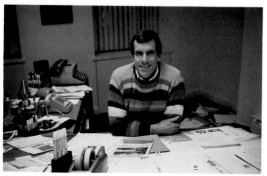

Fluorescent light plus FL filter

Fluorescent light presents a special problem because the color balance does not match either daylight or tungsten films, and it also depends on the type of fluorescent tube and its age. The light often gives an unpleasant greenish cast to pictures (left). Film manufacturers provide filtration data for different tubes but, practically speaking, the photographer usually doesn't know which tube is installed. Try an FL (fluorescent) filter with 1 stop increase in exposure (right). Daylight film will give a better balance than tungsten film if you use no filter.

CHANGES IN COLOR BALANCE:
TIME OF DAY/WEATHER

Have you ever had a picture come out an unexpected color even when you used the correct film? Perhaps a snowy scene in the shade turned out too blue, or a beach scene at sunset looked too orange. If you have, you may know how easy it is to fool the eye when it comes to color balance. Film that is manufactured to render colors accurately in the relatively blue light (high color temperature) at noon, will show colors differently if the color temperature shifts even slightly, for example, as it gets lower and more reddish at sunset.

Color temperature outdoors varies at different times of day and so produces different color balances on film. You'll find these shifts easier to notice if you are looking for them. Before dawn, colors are grayed and monochromatic. As the sun comes up, colors begin to stand out more clearly.

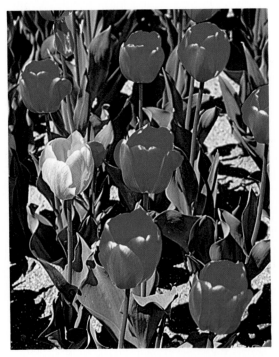

On a sunny day at noon, pictures tend to have clear, bright colors that snap out sharply.

But they appear more reddish than they will later in the day because in the early morning the color temperature of the sun's rays is modified as the rays travel a long distance through the earth's atmosphere.

Daylight-balanced film is designed for the color temperature of sunlight between about 10 A.M. and 2 P.M. During these hours, when the sun is most directly overhead, its rays are modified least by the atmosphere. Colors appear bright, clear, and accurate.

At sunset, the rays are again changed by the atmosphere. Blue rays are filtered out, leaving a surplus of reddish rays that turn color pictures taken at this time a warm, reddish-orange color. This reddish cast may be acceptable with some subjects; wood and skin tones usually appear natural even when the color temperature has shifted considerably to reddish-orange. But other subjects do not work as well; in a snowy winter scene photographed at sunset, the snow may turn an unnatural pink that merely looks odd. At dusk, colors are muted again and gradually become grayed and monochromatic as they were before dawn.

Atmospheric conditions also affect color balance. In the fog, snow, or rain, or on a heavily overcast day, colors are often muted. On these days, the farther away objects are from the camera, the more their colors are toned down. Sometimes a colored object in the foreground appears particularly bright because it is seen against a grayed background. ∎

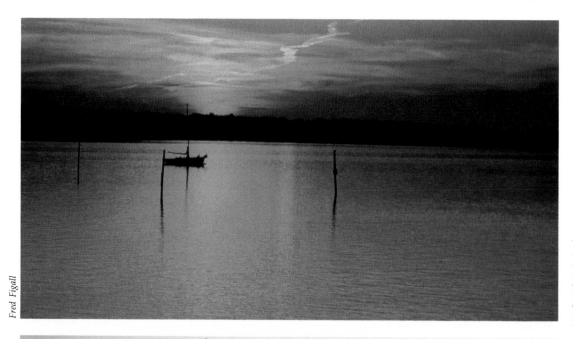

Fred Figall

At sunset, colors take on a reddish cast. Objects, and even skin tones, may appear quite orange but still pleasing.

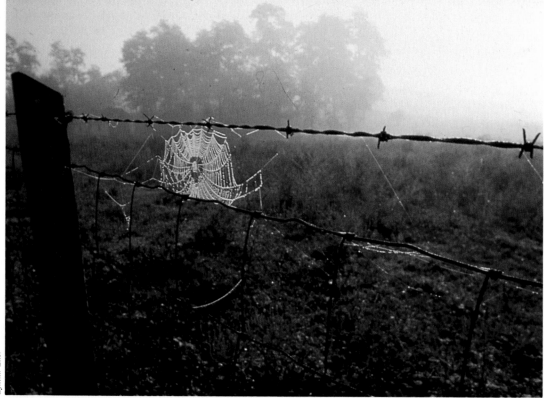

Lyntha Eiler

On a foggy day, colors are grayed and softened, particularly in the background. The color balance of pictures will be different under different atmospheric and light conditions.

UNEXPECTED COLORS: BLUE SHADOWS/VERY LONG EXPOSURES

The eye and brain quickly adapt to changes in color balance, especially if they have nothing to compare a color to directly; they tend to see a color as they expect it to be rather than as it is. If you know a dress to be white, your eye and brain see it as white even though it may have a distinctly green cast because of color reflected from grass or trees nearby. Color film is very sensitive to shifts in color balance and can produce unexpected results in the final picture if you are not watching for color casts when you shoot.

Shadow areas often appear bluer in color photographs than we expect them to be. On a sunny day, we tend to see shadows as simply dark, but they are receiving illumination from the indirect and very blue light of the sky. Color portraits taken in the shade (which provides a soft, pleasing modeling of facial features) often have better color balance if a UV (ultraviolet) or 1A (skylight) filter is used to eliminate some of the excess blue that is not always complimentary to skin tones.

Very long exposures (1 second or longer) cause shifts in color balance that can't be seen or even anticipated very well. During long exposures, film responds more slowly than usual (the reciprocity effect) and you may find your pictures underexposed as a result. In addition, the fact that each of the three layers of film emulsion responds at a different rate causes color balance to shift as well (see opposite).

To prevent underexposure with times of 1 second or longer, increase the exposure as explained on page 58. Color shifts can add interest to sunsets and other pictures, but if you wish to minimize them during long exposures, see the manufacturer's information sheet packed with the film for filters you can use. ▪

A portrait taken outdoors in the shade can have a slightly blue cast (left). A UV (ultraviolet) or a 1A (skylight) filter will remove some of the blue; an 81A (yellow) filter will remove even more (right).

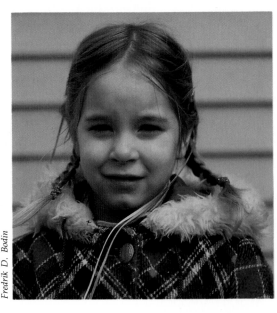

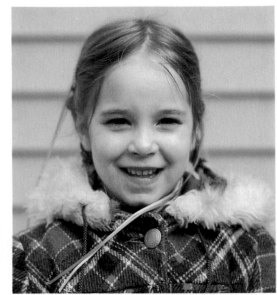

Fredrik D. Bodin

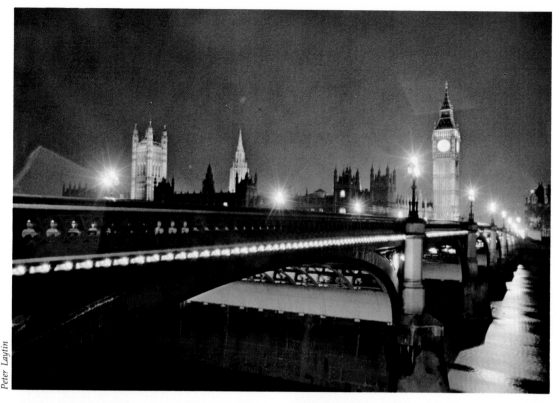

Peter Laytin

Unexpected colors can come from exposures of 1 second or longer. The longer the exposure, the more you are likely to get shifts in the color balance of the picture. A purple sky (below) was created when the photographer left the shutter open for several minutes at night in order to record lightning streaks. At left, a long exposure of a city scene at night produced an intensely yellow picture of a London bridge.

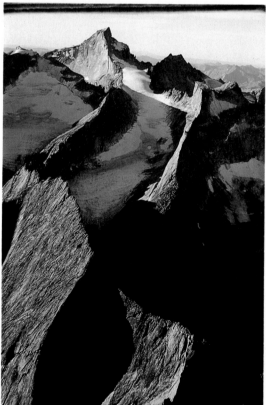

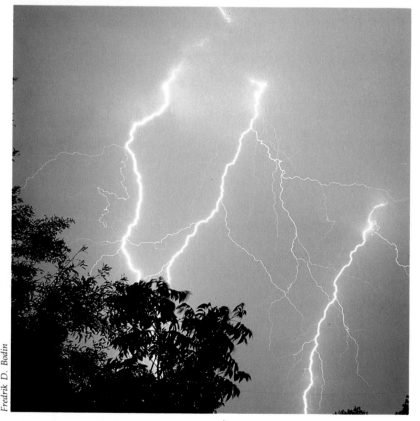

Fredrik D. Bodin

Blue shadows outdoors cause one of the unexpected colors often found in color photographs. The shadows on the snow are obviously blue in the photograph above, but were not so easy to see when the picture was taken. See also photograph opposite, left.

USING DARK SHADOWS

Deep, dark shadows can be a problem, particularly in color slides, because, as explained on page 63, a color slide has only abut ½ stop leeway in exposure. If you underexpose an important area in a color slide by more than ½ stop it will become significantly darker; it may be totally black if underexposed by several stops. But you can use this effect deliberately if you wish, in slides and in other photographs, silhouetting an interesting shape against a lighter background or accenting a brightly lit area that is of interest to you by surrounding it with a mass of dark shadows. ▪

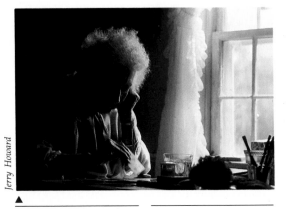

Jerry Howard

▲

A portrait half in shade can be made by metering and exposing for the lit side of the face when the shaded side of the face is much darker.

A silhouette against a ▶ sunset sky was made by metering the brightness of the sky (without including the sun) to calculate the exposure.

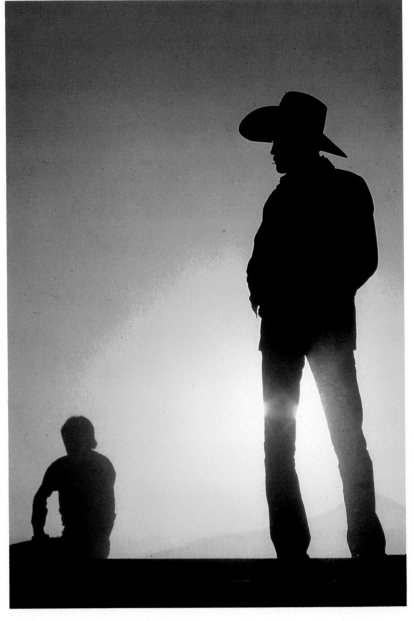

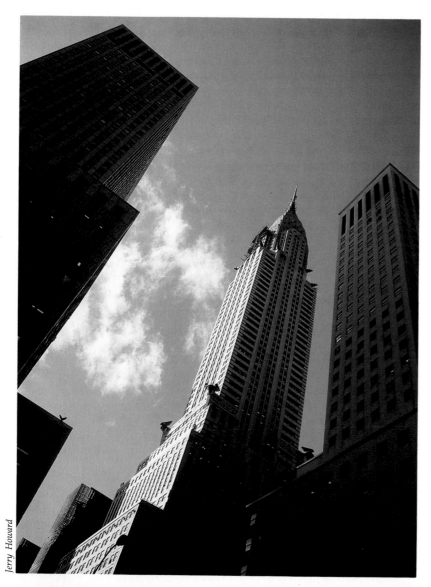

Jerry Howard

Silhouetting a subject against the sky can happen unintentionally if you include a bright sky in your meter reading. In the picture below of Natural Bridges National Monument, the photographer deliberately metered the sky for the exposure. The rock formation was several stops darker than the sky and thus was so much underexposed it appeared as almost black. At left, the dark shapes formed by the shaded sides of the building add interest to this city scene.

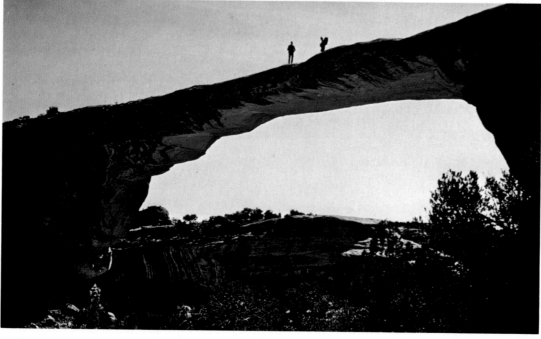

Fred E. Mang, Jr.

Chapter 5
· SPECIAL TECHNIQUES ·

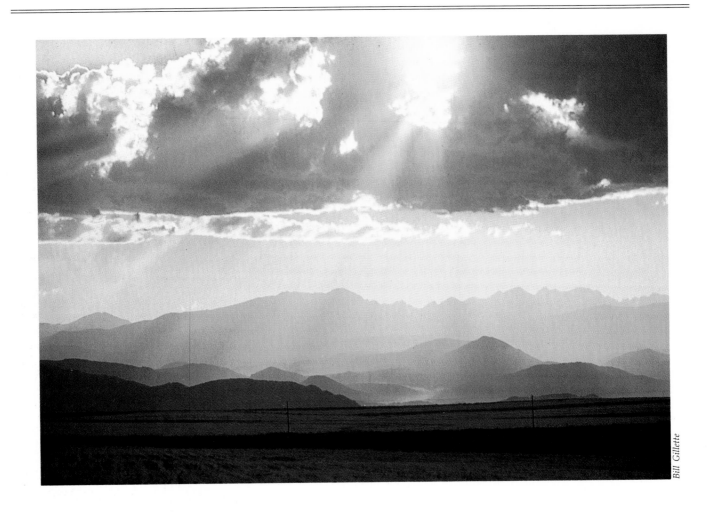

Bill Gillette

Many special techniques and manipulations are possible with photography. This chapter concentrates on two major areas: close-ups and the use of lens attachments and filters.

Close-ups We are used to seeing and photographing things from viewing distances of several feet or more. But many subjects—a tiny insect, the swirling petals of a flower—have a beauty and intricacy that are seen best from up close. Filling the entire picture with a detail of an object can reveal it in a new and unusual way.

The single-lens-reflex is an excellent camera for close-up work because you view the scene through the lens and see the exact image that the lens does (cameras without through-the-lens viewing show a different viewfinder angle than the one the lens projects on the film). Depth of field is usually very shallow when you photograph up close, and an SLR lets you preview which parts of the close-up will be sharp. Through-the-lens metering helps you calculate exposures accurately when using close-up accessories like extension tubes or bellows that decrease the amount of light reaching the film. Pages 80–83 tell more about close-ups and how to make them.

Lens attachments and filters A single-lens-reflex is also a good choice if you want to use lens accessories like cross-screen or multiple-image attachments. As you view the scene you can adjust the attachment right on the lens until you get just the effect you want. The next pages show some of these lens attachments and explain how to use filters that change colors and contrast. ▪

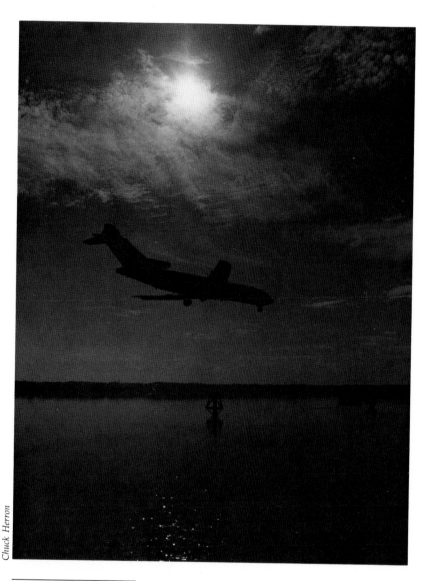

Chuck Herron

Moonlight effect Tungsten-balanced film will produce an image that is too blue for most pictures if it is shot in daylight without a filter to convert the light balance from a daylight color temperature to a tungsten color temperature (as shown on page 65). But if you shoot without a filter and also underexpose the film, you get an effect that looks very much like a moonlit scene. Daylight film with an 80B blue filter produces a similar effect.

USING FILTERS: HOW TO CHANGE FILM'S RESPONSE TO LIGHT

Filters for color photography Filters are often used in color photography to match the color balance of the light to that of the film so that the resulting picture looks more realistic. Using an FL (fluorescent) filter, for example, decreases the greenish cast of pictures taken under fluorescent light (shown on page 65). Or you can use filters to make a color photograph depart from reality, as, for example, in the arctic scene below. Various filters for color photography are listed in the chart opposite.

Filters for black-and-white photography Most black-and-white films are panchromatic—sensitive to all colors to about the extent that the human eye is. However, blue colors tend to record somewhat lighter than we expect them to in black-and-white photographs, and one of the most common uses of filters is to darken a blue sky

so that clouds stand out more distinctly (shown opposite). The chart opposite, bottom lists some of the filters used in black-and-white pictures.

Increasing exposures when filters are used Filters work by removing some of the wavelengths of light that pass through them. To compensate for the resulting overall loss of light intensity, the exposure must be increased or the film will be underexposed. Cameras with through-the-lens meters can measure the light through a filter on the lens, and, in most cases, will adjust the exposure as needed. Some types of meter cells may be more sensitive to certain colors than others, so check your owner's manual for special instructions. If you do not have a through-the-lens meter, increase the exposure manually as suggested by the filter manufacturer or as listed in the charts opposite. ▪

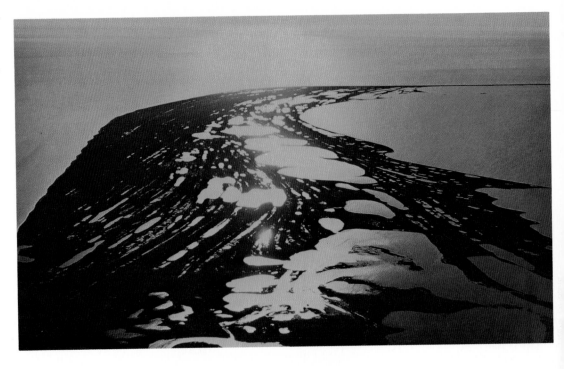

Color generates an emotional response and an unexpected color can make an image strikingly unusual. An orange filter was used for this arctic scene.

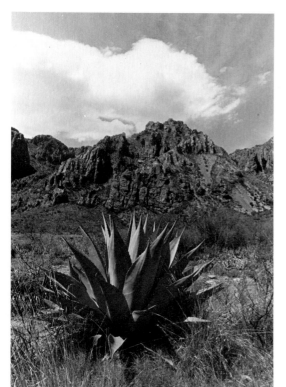

▲

A blue sky may appear very light in a black-and-white photograph because film is sensitive to the blue and ultraviolet light present in the sky.

A deep yellow filter was used on the camera lens for the black-and-white photograph below to darken the blue sky and make the clouds stand out.

▼

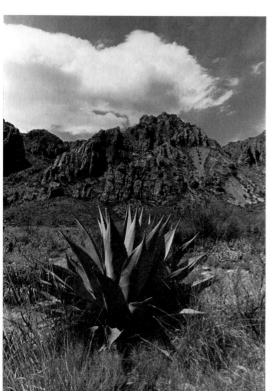

Filters for color film

	Type of filter	Increase needed in exposure
To get a natural color balance with daylight-balanced film exposed in tungsten light.	80A (blue) with photolamps	2⅓ stops
	80B (blue) with ordinary tungsten bulbs	2 stops
To get a natural color balance with tungsten-balanced film exposed in daylight.	85B (amber) with day-light-balanced film	⅔ stop
	85A (amber) with Type A film	⅔ stop
To get a natural color balance with fluorescent light.	FL-B with tungsten-balanced film	1 stop
	FL-D with daylight-balanced film	1 stop
To reduce the bluishness of light on overcast days or in the shade. To penetrate haze. Used by some photographers to protect lens.	1A (skylight)	No increase
	UV (ultraviolet)	No increase
To decrease bluishness more than 1A or UV.	81A (yellow)	⅓ stop
To decrease the red-orange cast of light at sunset and sunrise.	82A (blue)	⅓ stop
To balance film precisely as recommended by film manufacturer.	CC (color compensating): R (red), G (green), B (blue), Y (yellow), M (magenta), C (cyan)	Varies
To experiment with color changes.	Any color	Varies

Filters for black-and-white film

		Type of filter	Increase needed in exposure
To darken blue objects to:	Natural effect	8 (yellow)	1 stop
Make clouds stand out against blue sky.	Darker	15 (deep yellow)	1⅓ stops
Reduce haze in distant landscapes.	Very dark	25 (red)	3 stops
Make blue water darker in marine scenes (effect shows if sky is blue).	Darkest	29 (deep red)	4 stops
To increase haze for atmospheric effects in landscapes. To lighten blues to show detail, as in flowers.		47 (blue)	2⅔ stops
To lighten reds to show detail, as in flowers.		25 (red)	3 stops
To lighten greens to show detail, as in foliage.		58 (green)	2⅔ stops
To make the range of tones on panchromatic black-and-white film appear more like the range of brightnesses seen by the eye.		8 (yellow) with daylight	1 stop
		11 (yellow-green) with tungsten light	2 stops

LENS ATTACHMENTS: POLARIZATION, STARS, AND OTHER EFFECTS

A polarizing screen can remove reflections. If you have ever tried to photograph through a store window and seen more of the reflections from the street than whatever you wanted to photograph on display inside the store, you know how distracting unwanted reflections can be. Using a polarizing screen is a way to eliminate some of these reflections. The screen eliminates or decreases reflections from glass, water, or any smooth nonmetallic surface.

When shooting landscapes, using a polarizing screen makes distant objects clearer. The effect is strongest when you are shooting at a 90° angle to the sun.

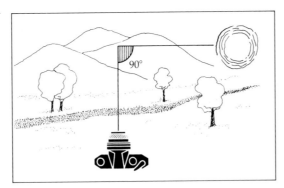

A polarizing screen removes reflections from surfaces such as glass (see illustrations opposite). The screen works best at a 30°–40° angle to the reflecting surface.

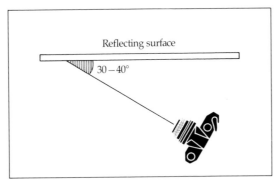

Reflecting surface

30 – 40°

Landscapes can be sharper and clearer with a polarizing screen. Light reflected from minute particles of water vapor or dust in the atmosphere can make a distant landscape look hazy and obscured. A polarizing screen will decrease these minute reflections and allow you to see more distant details. It may also help to make colors purer and more vivid by diminishing unwanted coloring such as reflections of blue light from the sky.

The screen works best at certain angles to your subject (see diagrams this page). The screen attaches like a filter to the front of the camera lens. With an SLR you can look through the viewfinder and adjust the screen until you get the effect you want. An exposure increase of 1 to 2 stops is usually required.

Special effects with lens attachments Stars of light in your photographs? Multiple images of a clump of wildflowers recorded several times on the negative or slide with just one exposure? In addition to the filters that change tone or color, other lens attachments manipulate or change the image itself. They can add drama to an otherwise ordinary picture, blur details to make an image soft and romantic, or change a scene in other unusual ways. If you take one or two along in your camera bag you might find uses for them that you hadn't expected. See the lens attachments illustrated on the following pages. ▪

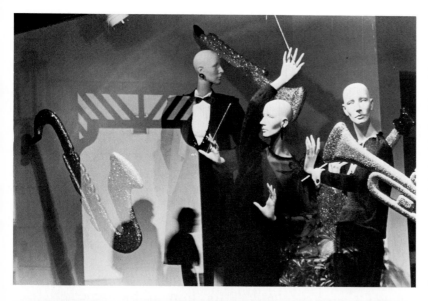

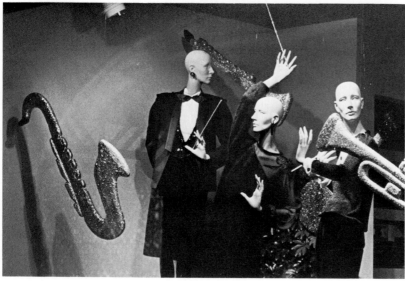

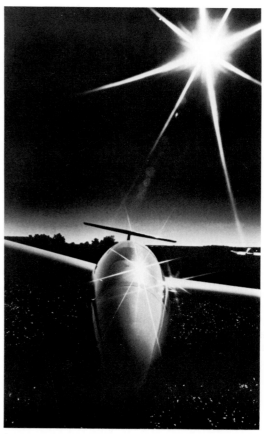

▲
A cross-screen lens attachment, sometimes called a star filter, put the bright stars of light in the photograph above. An eight-ray attachment created the rays around the sun and its reflections from the airplane. Other cross screens produce four, six, or other numbers of rays.

Reflections are a distracting element in the top photograph if the goal is to show the display inside the shop window. A polarizing screen on the camera lens removed most of the reflections in the bottom photograph so that the objects inside can be seen clearly. You may not always want to remove reflections, however; notice how the people reflected in the top photograph can be seen as an interesting addition to the picture.

LENS ATTACHMENTS
FOR SPECIAL EFFECTS

		Without attachment	With attachment

Soft focus

Softens details and can make bright highlights shimmer and gleam.

 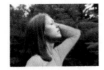 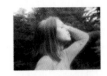

Spot lens

A sharp central field becoming progressively hazy at the edges. For emphasizing details of a subject.

 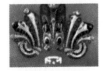 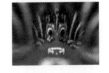

Prism 3X (triangular)

Triangular prism without a central image.

 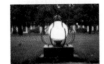 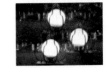

Prism 3X (parallel)

Multiple prism with three parallel fields. Reproduces the subject side by side, tilted, or one above the other.

 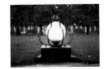 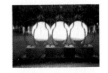

Prism 5X

A central field and four marginal sectors give a five-image reproduction.

  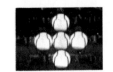

Prism 6X

Image is reproduced six times with five images arranged around a central field.

 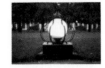 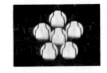

Color prism 3X (parallel)

Three parallel fields with colors changing gradually from yellow to green, blue, and purple.

 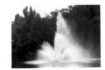 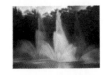

Color prism 6X

Pentagonal arrangement of five fields around the center field, with same color changes as above.

 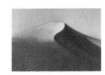 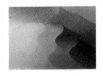

		Without attachment	With attachment

Prism 6X (Parallel)

The subject is repeated six times with one large image and five adjacent, parallel ones.

 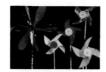 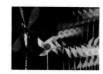

Close-up prism

Makes a close-up of a small object while at the same time doubling it—side by side, one above the other, or at parallel angles.

 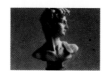 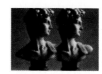

Split field or bifo

Part of the filter surface is a close-up lens and the rest is clear glass. Thus objects at close range (approx. 10 in. or 24 cm) and those far away can be focused sharply at the same time.

 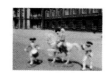 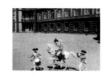

Eccentric spot lens

An off-center split field allows both a distant object and a very close one to be focused sharply.

 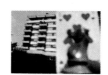 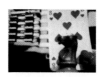

Cross screen (four-ray, six-ray, eight-ray)

Each point source—a point of bright light or bright reflection—radiates rays of light.

 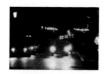 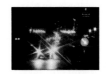

Spectra (4X, 8X)

Each point source of light radiates starlike beams in three spectral colors. Especially visible in night scenes.

 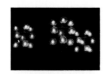 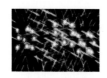

Spectra (2X)

Parallel beams of spectral colors emanate from every point light source.

 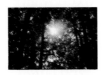 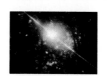

Spectra (48X)

Petal-shaped spectral beams around each point light source.

 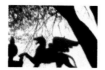 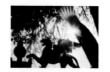

Spectra (72X)

Color spectra emanate from each point light source.

 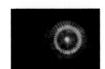 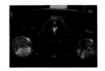

CLOSE-UPS:
BIGGER AND BETTER

Close-up equipment Shown opposite are the different types of close-up equipment you can use to produce a larger-than-normal image on your negatives. All of them do the same thing: they let you move in very close to the subject you are photographing.

Whether to use a camera support like a tripod depends on what and where you are photographing. You will be more mobile without one—ready to photograph an insect that has just alighted on a branch or to get down very close to a low-growing wildflower. However, close-up exposures are often longer than normal, and a tripod helps prevent blur caused by camera motion with a slow shutter speed. Also, a tripod lets you compose your pictures precisely, perhaps keeping the scene framed just as you want it while you meter it or arrange the lighting.

Increased exposures for close-ups
Placing extension tubes or bellows between the lens and the camera body lets you move in close to a subject, but the farther the lens gets from the camera, the dimmer the light that reaches the film. Beyond a certain extension the exposure must be increased or the film will be underexposed. A camera that meters through the lens increases the exposure automatically if compatible extension tubes or bellows are used. But if your camera does not meter through the lens or if the close-up attachment breaks the automatic coupling between lens and camera, you must increase the exposure manually. To do so, follow the recommendations given by the manufacturer of the tubes or bellows, or see the chart, opposite, below. Close-up lenses (see opposite) do not require an exposure increase. ▪

Close-up terms The closer your camera is to a subject, the larger the image on the film. A close-up is any picture taken from closer than normal to the subject—specifically, when the image on the film ranges from about 1/10 life size (1:10) to as big as life size (1:1). Macrophotography generally refers to an image on film that is anywhere from life size (1:1) to as big as ten times life size (10:1). Photomicrography, photographing through a microscope, is usually used to get a film image larger than 10:1.

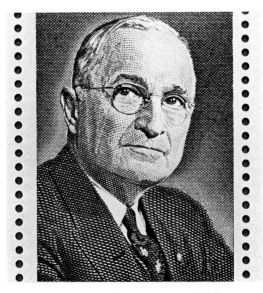

Life size (1:1) on film, enlarged to 2X life size here

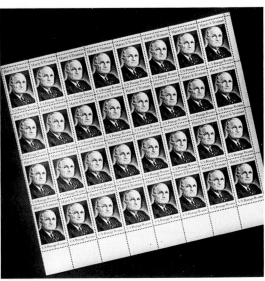

1/10 life size (1:10) on film, enlarged to 1/4 life size here

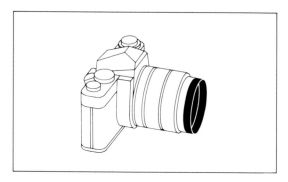

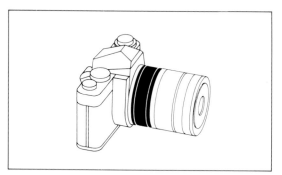

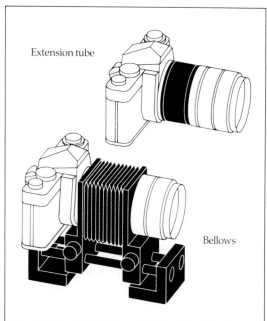

Extension tube

Bellows

A close-up lens attaches to the front of a camera lens and lets you focus up close without using extension tubes or bellows. Close-up lenses come in different strengths (diopters); the stronger the diopter, the closer you can focus and the larger the image. Close-up lenses are relatively inexpensive, small, and easy to carry along in your camera bag, and they do not require additional exposure as do extension tubes or bellows. However, image quality may not be as good as with other close-up methods.

A macro lens is your best choice for sharp close-ups. It produces a very sharp image at close focusing distances, whereas an ordinary lens produces its sharpest image at normal distances. A macro lens's mount can be extended more than that of an ordinary lens, which means that even without the use of extension tubes or bellows it can produce an image up to about half life size (1:2).

Reversing a lens produces a sharper image when the lens is used very close to the subject. At a short focusing distance an ordinary lens is being used under conditions for which it was not designed and, as a result, image sharpness decreases; reversing the lens improves sharpness. An adapter ring couples the lens to the camera in reversed position.

Extension tubes and bellows fit between the lens and the camera. They increase the distance from the lens to the film; the greater this distance, the closer you can bring the lens to the subject. Extension tubes come in graduated sizes that can be used in various combinations to make close-ups of different sizes. A bellows is more adaptable than fixed-length tubes because it can be expanded to any length. Using either tubes or bellows requires increasing the exposure, as explained opposite.

Exposure increase needed for close-ups *

If the long side of the area being photographed measures in inches	11	5⅛	3¼	2¼	2	1¾	1⅜	1
in cm	28	13	8.5	5.75	5	4.5	3.5	2.5
Open lens aperture this number of f-stops	⅓	⅔	1	1⅓	1½	1⅔	2	2½
Or multiply exposure time by	1.3	1.6	2	2.5	2.8	3.2	4	5.7

*Increase applies to a lens of any focal length used with a 35mm camera.

MORE ABOUT CLOSE-UPS

Depth of field is shallow in close-ups. At very close focusing distances, as little as an inch or less of the depth in the scene may be sharp, and the closer the lens comes to the subject, the more the background and foreground go out of focus. Accurate focusing is essential or it may miss the subject altogether. Small apertures help by increasing the depth of field but they also increase the length of the exposure time. It may be necessary to use a tripod and, if you are photographing outdoors, to shield your subject from the wind to prevent its moving during the exposure.

Making the subject stand out from the background Since a close-up is usually one small object or part of an object, rather than an entire scene, it is important to have some way of making the object you are photographing stand out clearly from its background. If you move your camera around to view the subject from several different angles, you may find that from some positions the subject will blend into the background, while from others it becomes much more dominant. You can choose your shooting standpoint accordingly.

Shallow depth of field can be an asset in composing your picture. You can use it to make a sharp subject stand out distinctly from an out-of-focus background. Tonal contrast of light against dark, the contrast of one color against another, or the contrast of a coarse or dull surface against a smooth or shiny one can also make your close-up subject more distinct.

Depth of field is very shallow when a photograph is made close to a subject. Only the insect's head and upper body are in focus; the front and rear legs and even the tips of the antennae are not sharp. The shallow depth of field can be useful: since the sharply focused parts contrast with the out-of-focus areas, the insect stands out clearly from the foreground and background.

Fred Ward

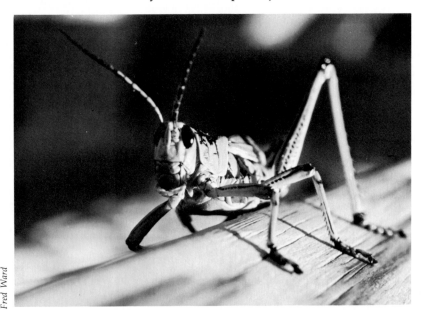

Lighting close-ups outdoors   Direct sunlight shining on a subject will be bright, and you can use smaller apertures for greater depth of field. But direct sunlight is contrasty, with bright highlights and very dark shadowed areas. Fill light helps to lighten the shadows if this is the case (pages 90–91). Light that comes from the back or side of the subject often enhances the subject by showing texture or by shining through translucent objects so they glow. In the shade or on an overcast day, the light is gentle and soft, good for revealing shapes and details.

Lighting close-ups indoors   You have more control over the lighting if you are arranging it yourself indoors, but stop for a moment and think about just what you want the lights to do. For flat subjects the lighting is not critical just so long as it is even. Two lights of equal intensity, each at the same distance and angle from the subject, will illuminate it uniformly.

If you want to bring out texture, one light angling across the subject from the side will pick out every ridge, fold, and crease. With a deeply textured object, you may want to add a second light close to the lens to add fill light so that important details are not lost in shadows.

Flash can be added to increase the light level if you need to use a smaller aperture or faster shutter speed, and you can also use flash as a fill light. Using the flash very close to the subject may make the light too bright; draping a handkerchief over the flash (out of the way of the camera lens) will soften the light and decrease its intensity. ▪

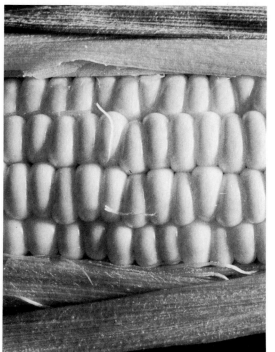

Stanley Rowin

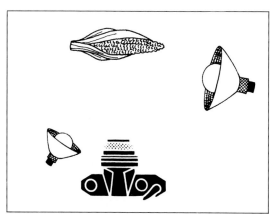

Cross lighting brought out the texture and volumes of this ear of corn. The main light angled across the subject from one side, while a weaker fill light close to the camera lightened the shadows.

Chapter 6
· LIGHTING ·

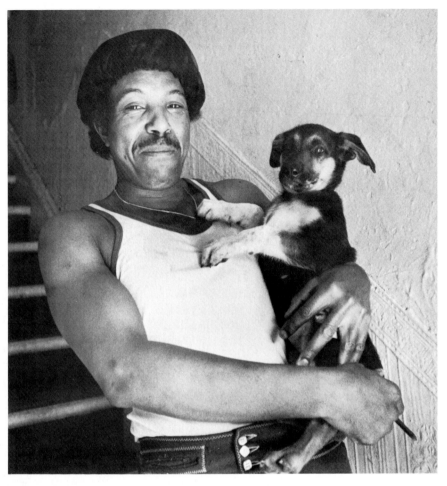

Jonas Dovydenas

Changes in lighting will change your picture. Outdoors, if clouds darken the sky or you change position so that your subject is lit from behind or you move from a bright area to the shade, your pictures will change as a result. Light changes indoors, too: your subject may move closer to a sunny window or you may turn the overhead lights on or decide to use flash lighting.

Changes in lighting affect the exposure of your film and the color balance of the light (important with color films). Just as important, the light can affect the feeling of the photograph so that the subject appears, for example, brilliant and crisp, hazy and soft, stark, romantic, or any of many other ways. If you make a point of observing the light on your subject, you will soon learn to predict how it will look in your photographs and you will find it easier to use existing light to arrange the lighting yourself to give just the effect you want. ▪

Look at the light on your subject. Soft, diffuse light bouncing in from outdoors softly lit a man and his dog just inside a doorway, opposite. A father and daughter on a crabbing expedition (right) are darkly silhouetted against reflections from water. Light can be as important a part of the picture as the subject itself.

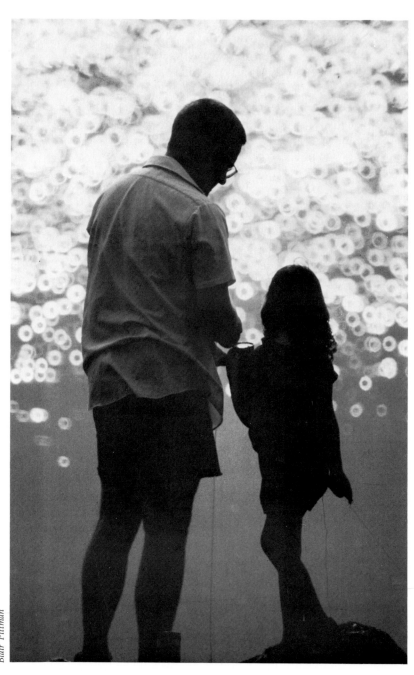

Blair Pittman

QUALITIES OF LIGHT: FROM DIRECT TO DIFFUSED

Whether indoors or out, light can range from direct and contrasty through many intermediate levels to diffuse and soft. Here's how to predict where you will find these different qualities of light and how they will look in your photograph.

Direct light is high in contrast. It creates bright highlights and dark shadows with sharp edges. Photographic materials, particularly color slides, cannot record details in very light and very dark areas at the same time; so in a slide the colors in directly lit areas will appear brilliant and bold while shadowed colors may turn out almost black. If you are photographing in direct light, you may want to add fill light (pages 90–91) to lighten shadows. Because the direct light probably will be quite intense, you can use a small aperture to give plenty of depth of field, a fast shutter speed to stop motion, or both, if the light is bright enough. The bright sun on a clear day is a common source of direct light. Indoors, a flash or photolamp pointed directly at your subject (that is, not bounced off another surface) also provides direct light.

Diffused light is low in contrast. It bathes subjects in light from all sides so that shadows are weak or even absent. Colors are less intense than they are in direct light and are likely to be pastel or muted in tone. Since the light will be less intense than direct

light, you might not be able to use a small aperture with a fast shutter speed. The sun on a heavily overcast day casts diffused light because the light is coming from the whole dome of the sky rather than just from the small disc of the sun. Indoors, diffused light can be created with a very large source of light used close to the subject (such as light bounced into a large umbrella reflector) plus additional fill light.

Directional/diffused light is intermediate in contrast. It is partly direct and partly diffused. Shadows are present, but they are softer and not as dark as in direct light. Colors are bright and more likely to be accurately rendered in both highlights and shadows. You will encounter this type of light on a cloudy day when the sun's rays are somewhat scattered so that light comes from the surrounding sky as well as from the sun. A shaded area, such as under trees or along the shady side of a building, can have directional/diffused light if the light is bouncing onto the scene primarily from one direction. Indoors, a skylight or other large window can give this type of light if the sun is not shining directly on the subject. Light from a flash or photolamp can also be directional/diffused if it is softened by a translucent diffusing material placed in front of the light or if it is bounced off another surface like a wall or an umbrella reflector. ■

Direct light

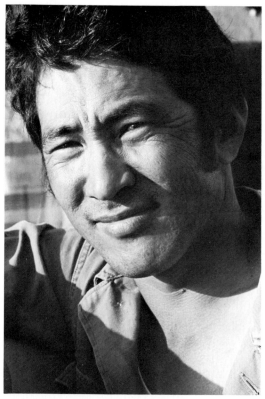

Bill Marr

Diffused light

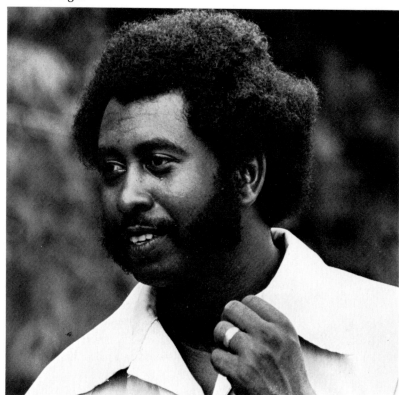

Michelle Bogre

Directional/diffused light

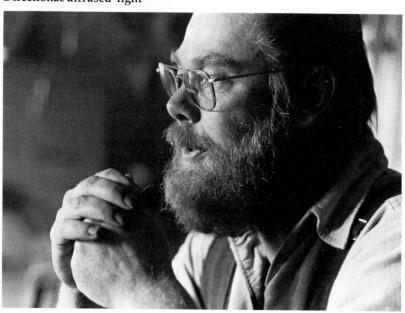

Charles O'Rear

Light changes—from place to place and at different times of day. Compare the qualities of the light in these portraits. Direct light (above, left)—hard edged and contrasty. Diffused light (above, right)—indirect and soft. Directional/diffused light (left)—softer-edged shadows.

THE MAIN LIGHT: THE STRONGEST SOURCE OF LIGHT

The most realistic and usually the most pleasing lighting resembles daylight, the light we see most often: one main source of light from above creating a single set of shadows. Lighting seems unrealistic (though there may be times when you will want that) if it comes from below or if it comes from two or more equally strong sources that produce shadows going in different directions.

Shadows create the lighting. Although photographers talk about the quality of light coming from a particular source, it is actually the shadows created by the light that can make an image harsh or soft, menacing or appealing. To a great extent the shadows determine the solidity or volume that shapes appear to have, the degree to which texture is shown, and sometimes the mood or emotion of the picture.

The main light, the brightest light shining on a subject, creates the strongest shadows. If you are trying to set up a lighting arrangement, look at the way the shadows shape or model the subject as you move the main light around or as you change the position of the subject in relation to a fixed main light.

Direct light from a 500-watt photolamp in a reflector was used for these photographs, producing shadows that are hard-edged and dark. Direct sunlight or direct flash can produce the same effects. The light would be softer if bounced onto the subject from another surface, like an umbrella reflector, or if it were diffused. Fill light (see next pages) will lighten the shadows. ▪

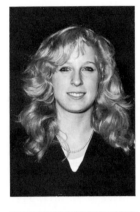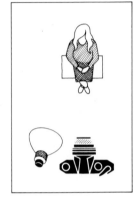

Front lighting Here the main light is placed close to the lens, as when a flash unit attached to the camera is pointed directly at the subject. Fewer shadows are visible from camera position with this type of lighting than with others, and, as a result, forms seem flattened and textures less pronounced. Many news photos and snapshots are front-lit because it is simple and quick to shoot with the flash on the camera.

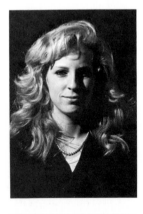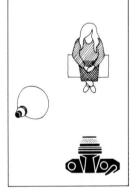

High 45° lighting If the main light is moved high and to the side of the camera, not precisely at 45° but somewhere in that vicinity, shadows model the face to a rounded shape and emphasize textures more than with front lighting. This is often the main light position used in commercial portrait studios; fill light would then be added to lighten the shadows.

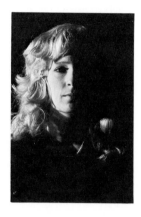 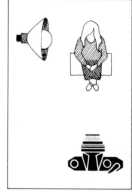 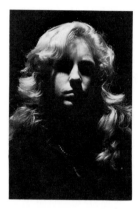 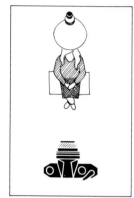

Side lighting A main light that is at about a 90° angle to the camera will light the subject brightly on one side and cast shadows across the other side. When the sun is low on the horizon at sunset or sunrise, it can create side lighting that adds interest to landscapes and other outdoor scenes. Side lighting is sometimes used by portrait studios to dramatize a subject.

Top lighting With the light directly overhead, long dark shadows are cast into eye sockets and under nose and chin, producing an effect that is seldom appealing for portraits. Unfortunately, top lighting is not uncommon—outdoors at noon when the sun is overhead or indoors when the main light is coming from ceiling fixtures. Fill light to open up the shadows will help.

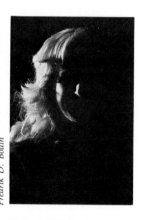 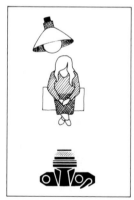 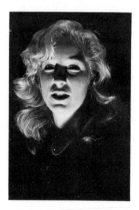 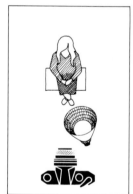

Frank L. Bodin

Back lighting Here the light is moved around farther to the back of the subject than it is in the photograph above. If the light were directly behind the subject the entire face would be in shadow with just the hair outlined by a rim of light. Outdoors, bright light that comes from behind the subject can silhouette it unless fill light from the front is used to lighten the shadows.

Bottom lighting Lighting that comes from below looks distinctly odd in a portrait. This is because light on people outdoors or indoors almost never comes from below. This type of light casts unnatural shadows that often create a menacing effect. Some products, however, like glassware, are effectively lit from below.

THE FILL LIGHT:
TO LIGHTEN SHADOWS

A sunny day is an inviting time to go photographing. But, particularly for portraits, bright, direct sunlight may create harsh, contrasty shadows that come out too dark in the final photograph. This can be corrected by adding fill light to lighten the shadows.

Fill light outdoors It is easier to obtain a pleasant expression on your subject's face in a sunlit outdoor portrait if your subject is lit from the side or from behind and is not squinting directly into the sun. However, this position may make the shadowed side of the face too dark. To decrease the contrast between the lit and shadowed sides of the face, fill light from a reflector or flash unit can be added, as illustrated below. Fill light is also used outdoors for close-ups of flowers or other relatively small objects in which the shadows would otherwise be too dark.

When do you need fill light? Photographic materials, particularly color slides, can successfully record color and texture in either brightly lit areas or in deeply shadowed ones, but not in both at the same time. So if important shadow areas meter more than one or two stops darker than highlight areas, consider whether adding fill light will improve your picture, especially if you are shooting color slides. The fill light should not overpower the main light but should simply raise the light level of shadow areas. ■

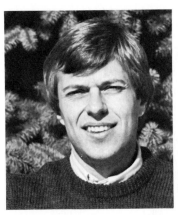

Front light The man's face is illuminated brightly by sunlight shining directly on it. But facing into the sun almost guaranteed an awkward squint against the bright light.

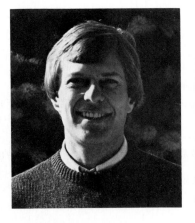

Back light Here he faces away from the sun and has a more relaxed expression. However, most of his face is now in shadow; it is dark in this print and would be even darker in a color slide. Increasing the exposure would lighten the shadowed side of his face but would make the lit side very light.

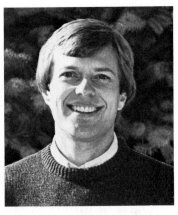

Back light plus fill light Here he still faces away from the sun, but to lighten the shadows the photographer has added fill light from a small flash unit on the camera.

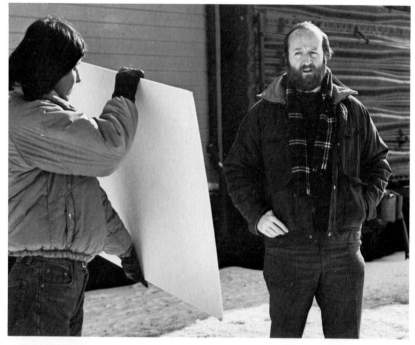

Using a reflector for fill light

A large light-colored cloth or card can lighten shadows in back-lit or side-lit portraits by reflecting back some of the illumination from the main light. For color photographs, the reflector should be neutral in color so that an unwanted color is not cast on the subject. Sometimes nearby objects will act as natural reflectors, for example, sand, snow, water, or a light-colored wall.

At left, an assistant holds the reflector for the photographer, but in many cases the reflector could simply be propped up. The closer the reflector is to the subject, the more light it will reflect into the shadows.

For a portrait, meter the lit side of the face to determine the basic exposure. Then try to angle the reflector to add enough fill light so the shadowed side of the face is about one stop darker than the sunlit side.

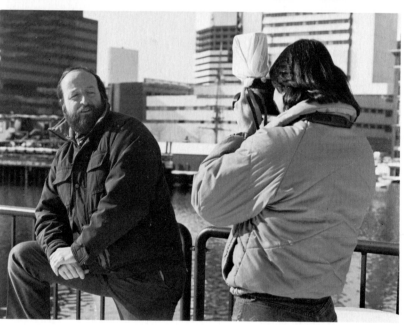

Alan Oransky

Using flash for fill light

To lighten the shadows on the man's face, the photographer at left has attached a flash unit to her camera. If the flash light is too bright it can overpower the main light and create an unnatural effect. To prevent this, the photographer has draped a handkerchief over the flash head to decrease the intensity of the light. She could also have stepped back from the subject or, with some units, decreased the light output of the flash.

See your owner's manual for instructions on how to set your camera and flash for fill lighting. In general, you will need to decrease the brightness of the flash on the subject until it is about one stop less than the basic exposure from the sun. Position the fill light close to the camera (attached to the camera is fine) so as not to cast a second set of shadows that will be visible from camera position.

USING ARTIFICIAL LIGHT: PHOTOLAMP OR FLASH

Artificial light sources let you bring your own light with you when the sun goes down or you move inside into a darkened room or you need just a little more light than is available naturally. Artificial sources are consistent and never go behind a cloud just when you're ready to take a picture. You can manipulate them to produce any effect you want—from light that looks like natural sunlight to underlighting that is seldom found in nature. Different sources produce light of different color balances, an important factor if you are using color films. See pages 64–65 for more about color balance and films.

Continuously burning lamps such as photolamps and quartz lamps plug into an AC electrical outlet. Since they let you see how the light affects the

subject, they are excellent for portraits, still lifes, and other stationary subjects that give you time to adjust the light exactly. Determining the exposure is easy: you meter the brightness of the light just as you do outdoors. The color balance of these lights is matched to two types of color film: the lamps emit either a 3200 K color temperature for use with tungsten-balanced color film or 3400 K for Type B film.

Flashbulbs are conveniently portable, powered by small battery units. Each bulb puts out one powerful, brief flash and then must be replaced. Press photographers not so many years ago could be followed by the trail of spent flashbulbs they left as they discarded a bulb after each shot. Flashbulbs are still in use for some special purposes and are also used with snapshot cameras that accept flashcube or flip-flash units. Flashbulbs are blue coated for use with daylight-balanced color film or are clear for tungsten-balanced film. Bulbs that put out only infrared light are also available.

Electronic flash or strobe is now the most popular source of portable light. Though initially more expensive than flashbulbs, it offers many repeated flashes without the need of replacing the bulb, so it is ultimately more economical. Power can come from either battery packs or an AC outlet. The color balance of electronic flash is best with daylight-balanced color film. Flash (from either an electronic flash or a flashbulb) is fast enough to freeze most motion; flash is therefore a good choice when you need to light candid or unposed shots.

(A) Flashbulb and reflector
(B) Flashcube
(C)(D) Electronic flash units
(E) Photolamp

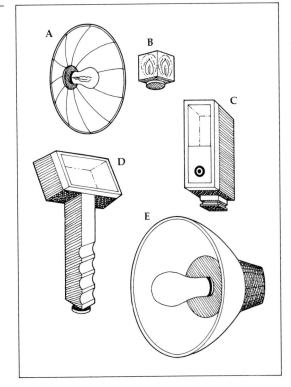

Flash must be synchronized with the camera's shutter so that the flash of light occurs when the shutter curtains are fully open. Only shutter speeds of 1/60 sec. or slower synchronize with electronic flash (up to 1/125 sec. with certain shutters). At faster shutter speeds the shutter curtains open only part of the way at any time and only part of the film would be exposed. See your owner's manual for details on how to set your camera.

Automatic flash units measure the amount of light reflected back from the subject during the flash, then terminate the flash when the exposure is adequate. Even if you have an auto-matic unit, there are times when you will want to calculate the flash exposure yourself, such as when the subject is very close to the flash or very far from it and so is not within the automatic flash range.

Determining your own exposure with flash is different from the procedure used with other light sources. The flash of light is too short to measure with an ordinary light meter. Instead, the intensity of the light is measured by the distance of the flash from the subject, and the aperture is set accordingly (see below). Changing the shutter speed (within the acceptable range) does not affect the exposure. ▪

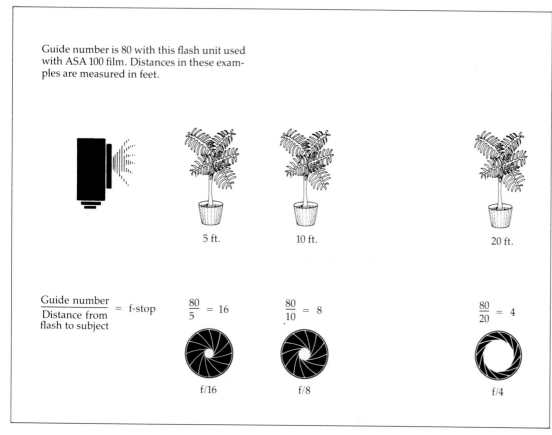

Guide number is 80 with this flash unit used with ASA 100 film. Distances in these examples are measured in feet.

5 ft.   10 ft.   20 ft.

$$\frac{\text{Guide number}}{\text{Distance from flash to subject}} = \text{f-stop}$$

$$\frac{80}{5} = 16 \qquad \frac{80}{10} = 8 \qquad \frac{80}{20} = 4$$

f/16   f/8   f/4

To set your own flash exposure, set the aperture according to how far your subject is from the flash: divide the distance from flash to subject into the guide number (a rating for the flash when used with a specific film speed); the result is the f-stop that should be used.

Flash units have a calculator dial that will do the division for you: dial in the film speed and the distance from the subject, and the dial will show the correct f-stop.

Notice that the farther the subject is from the flash, the dimmer is the light that it receives and so the larger the aperture opening that is needed to maintain the same exposure.

MORE ABOUT FLASH

Flash is easy to use for portrait lighting: the flash of light exposure is so fast that you don't have to worry about the subject moving during the exposure—particularly important with children—and you can expose at the instant your subject has the expression you want. Light from flash is so quick (1/1000 sec. or shorter) that you can't really see what the subject looks like when lit. However, with a little practice you can predict the qualities of light that are typical of different flash positions. Shown on the opposite page are some simple lighting setups for portraiture.

A few cautions with flash If you have the flash close to the lens and the sitter is looking directly at the camera, you may find that your subject's eyes appear red or amber in a color picture. This is because light is reflecting from the blood-rich retina inside the eye. The effect can be easily prevented by having the subject look slightly to one side or by holding the flash away from the camera. If your subject wears eyeglasses, this will also prevent bright reflections from them. Reflections from shiny backgrounds can be avoided with flash by shooting at an angle to them. ∎

Unwanted reflections When using flash you may fail to notice bright, distracting reflections caused by light bouncing back from reflective surfaces like shiny walls, mirror, or glass.

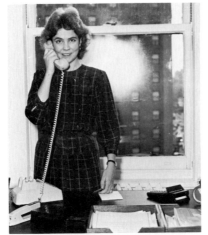 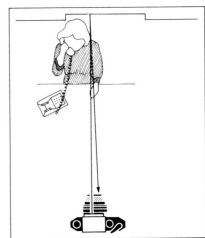

To avoid reflections with flash, shoot at an angle to highly reflective surfaces or move the flash to one side. The light will be reflected off at an angle instead of returning to the camera.

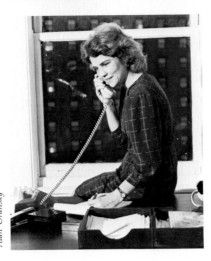 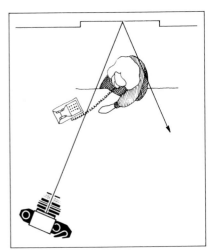

Alan Oransky

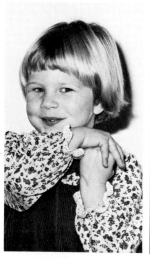 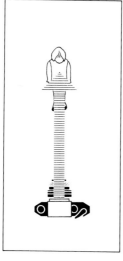 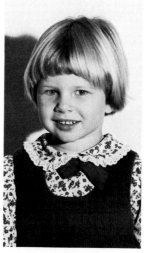 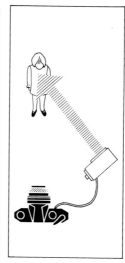

Direct flash on camera is simple and easy to use because the flash is attached to the camera. However, the light shining straight at the subject from camera position tends to flatten out roundness and gives the photograph a rather harsh look.

Direct flash off camera—usually raised and to one side—gives more roundness and modeling than does flash on camera. A special extension (synchronization or synch) cord lets you move the flash away from the camera. To avoid a shadow on the wall, move the subject away from it or raise the flash more.

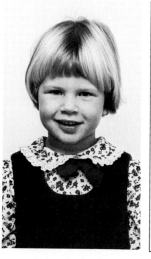 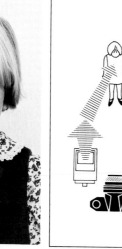 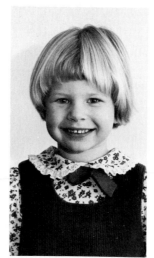 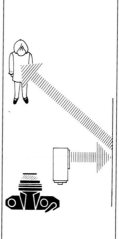

Alan Oransky

Flash bounced from the ceiling onto the subject gives a softer, more natural light than direct flash. Usually about 2 stops more exposure is needed than with direct flash from the same distance. Light can also be directed into an umbrella reflector and then bounced onto the subject.

Flash bounced from a side wall onto the subject gives a soft, flattering light. The closer the subject is to the wall, the more distinct the shadows on the subject will be. To avoid a shadow on the back wall, move the subject away from it.

Chapter 7
· SEEING LIKE A CAMERA ·

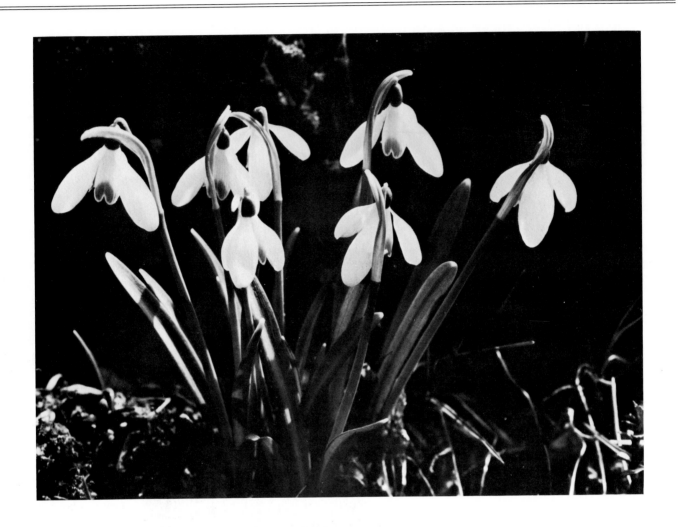

Pictures translate the world we see. If you have ever had a picture turn out to be different from what you anticipated, you know that the camera does not "see" the way a human sees. For example, in a black-and-white photograph the colors we see in the world are translated into shades of gray, but even color film does not record colors exactly the way the eye sees them, and a color print can alter colors even more.

The way we see contrast is also different from the way film responds to it. When we look at a contrasty scene, the iris of the eye continuously adjusts to different levels of brightness by opening up or closing down. In a photograph the contrast between very light and very dark areas is often too great for the film to record them both well in the same picture, so some areas may appear overexposed and too light or underexposed and too dark. Motion, sharpness, and other elements also can be similar to what we see in the original scene, but never exactly the same.

The creative part of photography is that you can choose the way you want the camera and film to translate a scene. You decide whether you want traffic to blur into a stream of lights. You decide whether you want the sky to be almost white or showing detail in clouds. You decide whether you want the flowers brightly lit against a very dark background. More about your choices—and how to make them—on the following pages. ▪

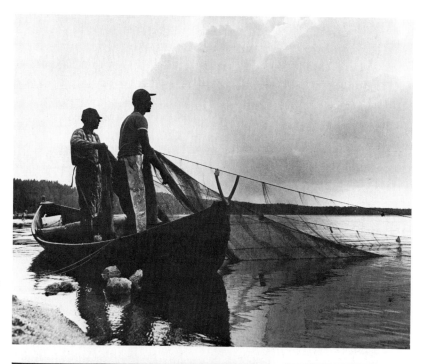

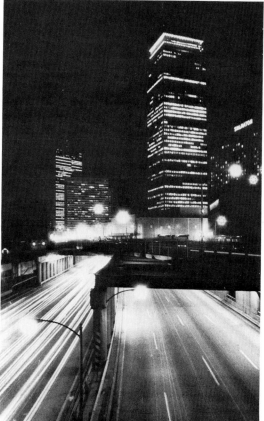

David A. Morrison

Choices During a 15 sec. exposure, lights on moving automobiles streaked (left). A shorter exposure would have made the streaks shorter and the roadway even darker. Above, the sky and water were brighter than the fishermen and their boat. More exposure would have made the whole scene lighter, revealing more of the people, but with the sky almost white. Opposite, the background was much darker than the flowers. With more light on the background or with more exposure, the background would have been more visible, but the flowers would not have stood out so strongly.

WHAT'S IN THE PICTURE:
THE EDGES OR FRAME

One of the first choices to make with a photograph is what to include and what to leave out. The image frame, the rectangle you see when you look through the viewfinder, shows only a section of the much wider scene that is in front of you. The frame crops the scene—or, rather, *you* crop it—when you decide where to point the camera, how close to get to your subject, what angle to shoot at—in other words, what to include in your picture.

Decide before you shoot whether you want to show the whole scene (or as much of it as you can) or whether you want to move in close for a detail. You can focus attention on something by framing it tightly or you can step back and have it be just another element in a larger scene. When you look through the viewfinder, imagine you are viewing the final print or slide. This will help you frame the subject better. The tendency is to "see" only the subject and ignore its surroundings. In the final print, however, the surroundings and the framing are immediately noticeable.

You can also change framing later by cropping the edges of a picture either when you print it yourself or when you send it to a lab to be printed. Many photographs can be improved by cropping out distracting elements at the edges of the frame. But if you are making slides, it is best to crop when you take the picture. Although you can duplicate a slide and change its cropping then, it's easier to frame the scene the way you want it when you shoot. ∎

The edges of a picture, the frame, surround and shape the image. Look around the edges at how the frame cuts into some objects or includes them in their entirety. How could different framings change these pictures?

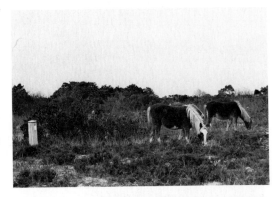 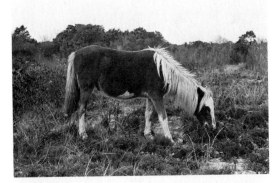

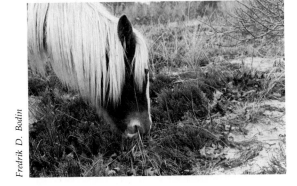 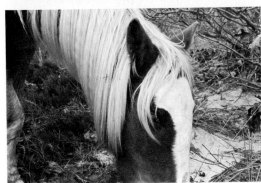

Fredrik D. Bodin

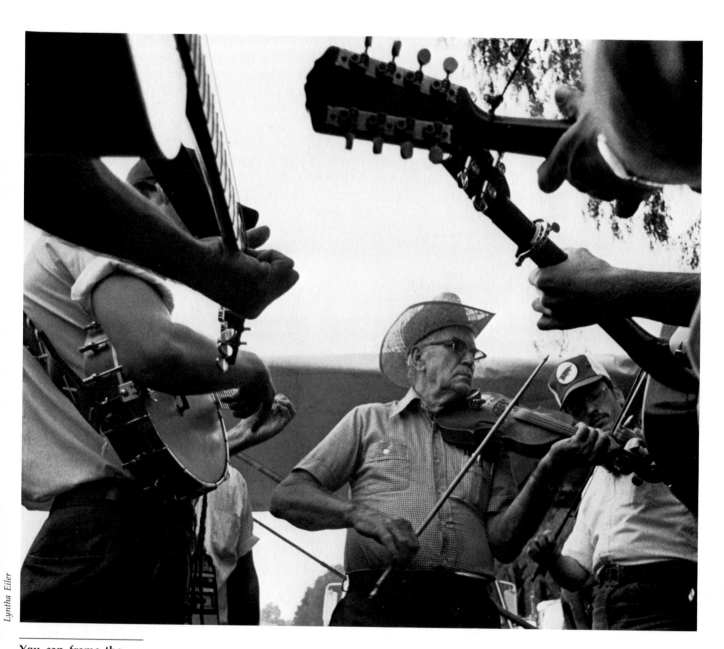

Lyntha Eiler

You can frame the central subject of a picture with other parts of the scene. Showing the instruments surrounding the fiddler at center, while cropping out most of the musicians themselves, focuses attention on the fiddler.

WHAT'S IN THE PICTURE:
THE BACKGROUND

Seeing the background When you view a scene, you see most sharply whatever you are looking at directly, and you see less clearly objects in the background or at the periphery of your vision. If you are concentrating on something of interest you may not even notice other things nearby. But the lens does see them, and it shows unselectively everything within its angle of view. Unwanted or distracting details can be ignored by the eye looking at a scene, but in a picture they are evident. To eliminate a distracting background, you can shoot the background out of focus (see page 104) or change your angle of view as in the photographs below. Interesting juxtapositions that usually go unnoticed—except in a photograph—are one of the pleasures of photography, as in the picture opposite. ▪

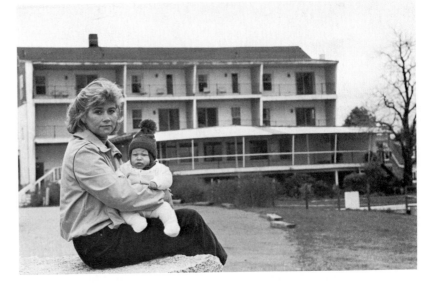

A distracting background of a building is an unnecessary element in this portrait. The woman and child also seem rather a small part of the picture.

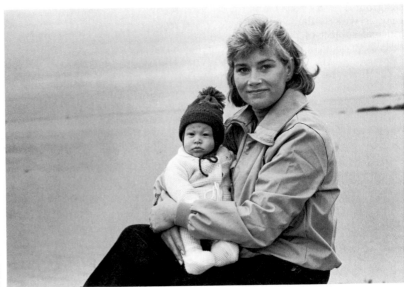

A plainer and better background resulted when the photographer simply walked around to one side and changed the angle from which he shot the subject. The photographer also moved in closer so that the people would occupy a larger area of the picture.

Fredrik D. Bodin

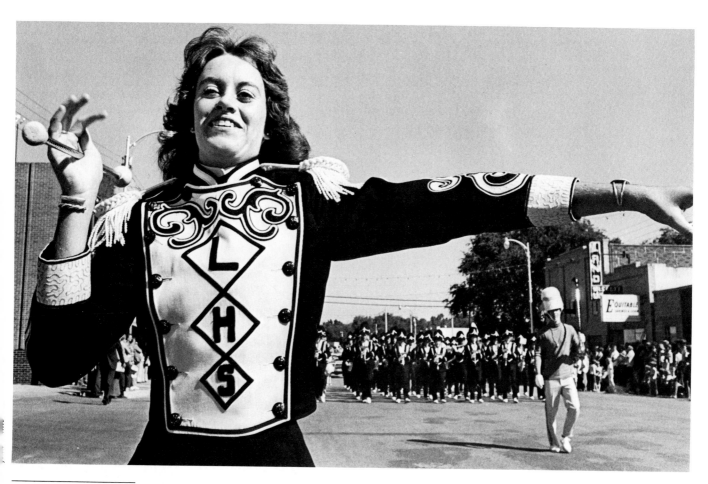

If you look at the background of a scene as well as the principal subject of interest, you may find some good combinations. Here, the leader of a high school band frames the rest of the band with her outstretched arm. The camera records everything within its angle of view and can make the relation between a foreground object and a background one more important than we might otherwise notice.

DEPTH IN A PICTURE: THREE DIMENSIONS BECOME TWO

Photographs can seem to change the depth in a scene. When you translate the three dimensions of a scene that has depth into the two dimensions of a flat photograph, you can expand space so that objects seem very far apart, or you can compress space so that objects appear to be crowded close together. For example, compare the two photographs below. You can compress the buildings in a city (opposite) into flat planes to look almost as if they were pasted one on top of the other, or you can give them exaggerated height. Pages 34–35 explain more about how to control perspective effects like these that can change the way a photograph shows depth. ▪

Two lenses of different focal lengths gave two very different versions of the same scene from the same position: a short-focal-length lens (top) expanded the space; a long-focal-length lens (bottom) compressed it. Neither of the lenses actually changed anything in the scene. The short-focal-length lens simply included nearby objects as well as those that were farther away. The part of the scene shown in the bottom photograph is exactly the same within the wider view of the scene shown in the top photograph.

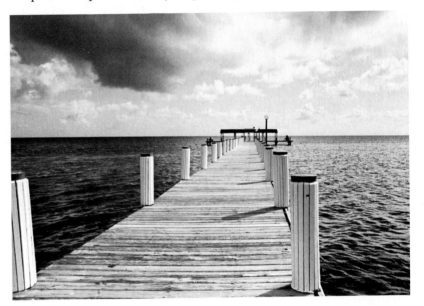

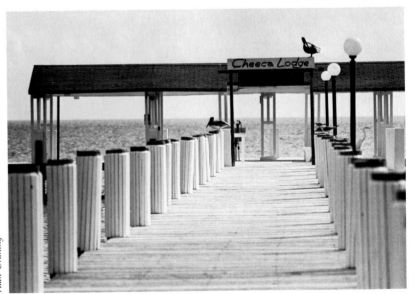

Alan Oransky

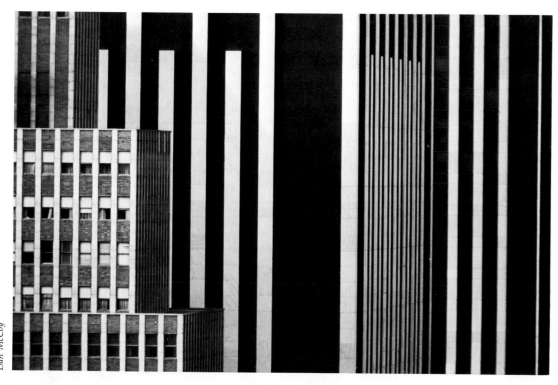

Dan McCoy

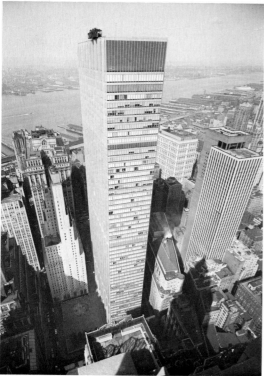

Two perspectives of the same city Buildings appear to tower to great heights when you look down on them (bottom). The closer any object is to your eye or to the camera, the bigger it appears to be, so the building looks larger at the top than at the bottom because the camera was closer to its top stories than to its bottom ones. Sections of buildings seen from the side seem to lie one right on top of the other (top). Clues that might indicate the actual space that exists between the buildings are all excluded from the scene.

DEPTH OF FIELD: WHICH PARTS ARE SHARP

We are usually not aware that we focus our eyes on only one distance at a time while objects at all other distances are not as sharp. Our eyes automatically adjust their focus as we look from one object to another. You might look at the butterfly in the scene opposite, bottom and not notice that you are not seeing the girl just on the other side of the window as clearly as you see the butterfly. But in a photograph, differences in the sharpness of objects at different distances are immediately evident. Such differences can be distracting or can add interest to the photograph.

Controlling the depth of field   In some photographs you have no choice about depth of field (the area within which all objects will appear acceptably sharp). For example, in dim light or with slow film or under other conditions, the depth of field may have to be very shallow. But usually you can control the depth of field to some extent, as shown on pages 30–31. It is not necessarily better to have everything totally sharp or the background out of focus—or to follow any other rules, but it is important to remember that in the photograph you will notice what is sharp and what isn't. ▪

Landscapes are often photographed with everything sharp from foreground to background. The entire landscape is important, not any single part of it. If you had been standing by the camera when this picture was taken, each part of the scene would have looked sharp to you. You wouldn't have noticed that your eyes were actually focusing sharply first on the fence in the foreground, then refocusing on the house in the middle distance, then focusing again on the mountains in the background.

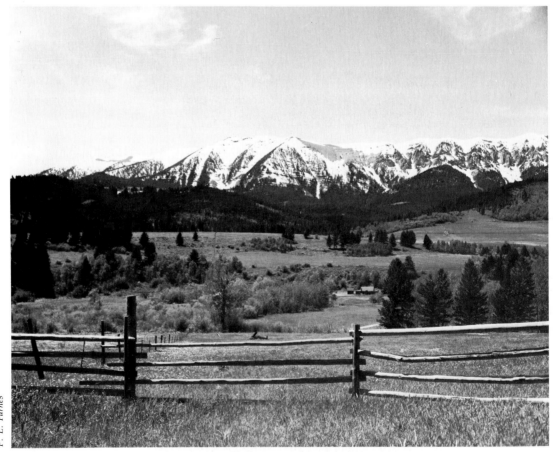

P. E. Farnes

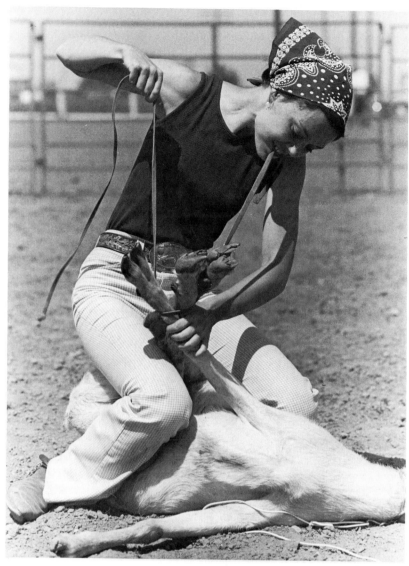

Throwing the background out of focus is one way to make a busy background less distracting. The eye tends to look first at the objects in a photograph that are the sharpest, and here the interesting part of the picture is the woman roping the calf, not the fence and the next corral in the background.

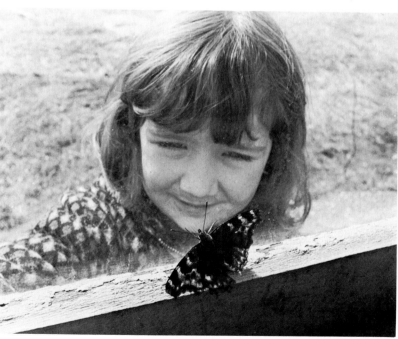

The most important part of the picture is usually—but not always—the one that is focused most sharply. With the butterfly very sharp and the girl slightly out of focus, the relationship between the two of them is emphasized even more than it would be if both of them were equally sharp.

TIME AND MOTION
IN A PHOTOGRAPH

A photograph is a slice of time. Just as you select the section that you want to photograph out of a larger scene, you can also choose the section of time you want to record. You can think of a photograph as slicing through time, taking a wide slice at a slow shutter speed or a narrow slice at a fast shutter speed. In that slice of time, things are moving, and, depending on the shutter speed, direction of the motion, and other factors dis-cussed earlier (pages 10–11), you can show objects frozen in mid-movement, blurred until they are almost unrecognizable, or blurred to any extent in between. How would you have photographed the rodeo scene (opposite, top)—sharp, as it is, or blurred to show the jolting of the bull? How about the boxers (below)—blurred and streaked or sharp and crisp to show their exact stances? ▪

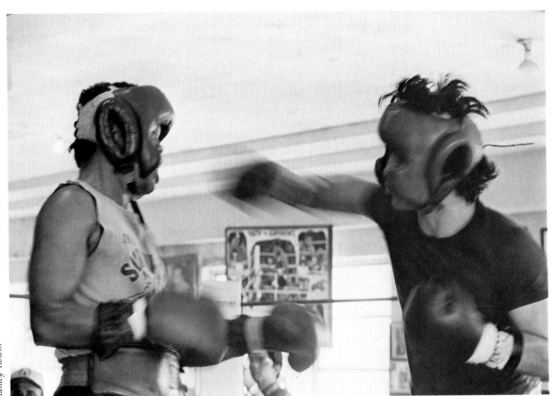

Stanley Rowin

A slow shutter speed blurred the boxers' fists, which were moving, while their torsos, which were relatively still, are sharper.

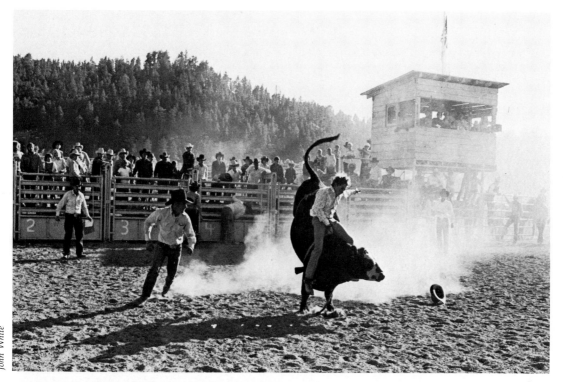

A fast shutter speed froze the motion of the bull, men, hat, and dust. With bright sunlight and a high film speed, the photographer was also able to use a small aperture so that everything is sharply focused from foreground to background.

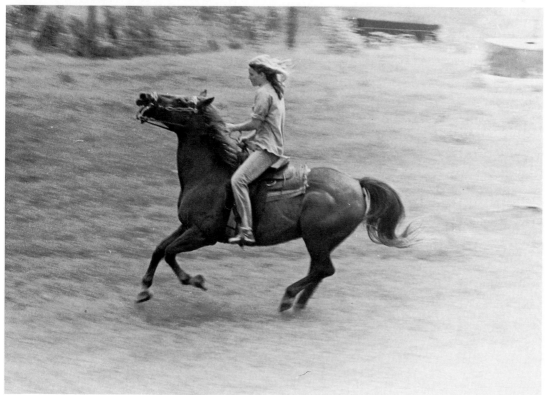

Panning, moving the camera in the direction that the subject is moving, is another way to show motion. The moving subject is relatively sharp while the surrounding scene is blurred.

PHOTOGRAPHING CHILDREN:
AT THEIR LEVEL

Children are probably the most photographed subjects in the world, but all too often photographers look down on them from adult height. If you can get down to children's level by kneeling, sitting, or doing whatever you have to, you and your photographs can participate more intimately in their world. You can also put children more at ease if you and your camera are at about their height rather than looming over them. ▪

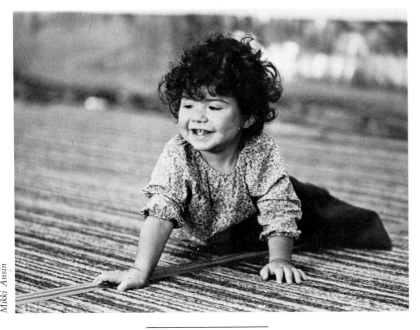

Mikki Ansin

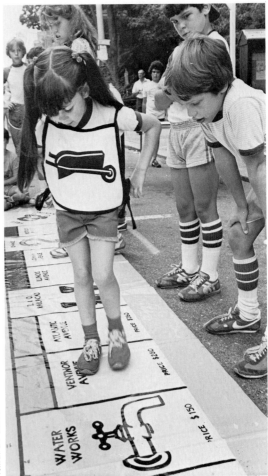

Fredrik D. Bodin

Shooting from a low level may show more of the background than if you shot down on a subject from above. Use a small aperture if the background adds interest to the picture and you want it sharp. Use a large aperture if you want the background out of focus and less noticeable.

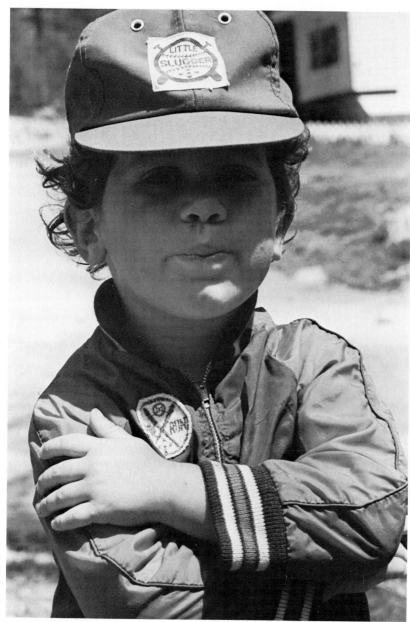

Fredrik D. Bodin

A person looking into the camera lens can be an effective way of conveying direct contact with your subject. These children seem at ease with the photographer and involved with the picture-making pro- cess. If you are physically at their level, children (and adults) may be more receptive to your presence than if you stare down at them so that they have to crane their necks to look up at you.

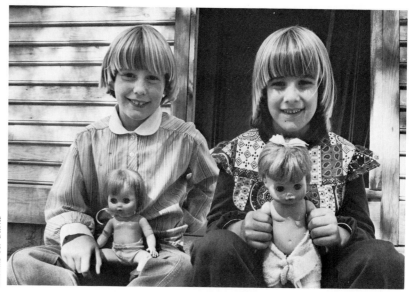

Thomas A. Burns

PHOTOGRAPHING CHILDREN: WHILE THEY ARE OCCUPIED

Photographing children when they are busy doing something besides being photographed is a good way to capture expressions that are natural and spontaneous. It pays to be familiar with the camera's controls so that you can operate them easily and quickly. Telling a child to "hold still" while you make last-minute adjustments is likely to produce a wooden smile at best. ▪

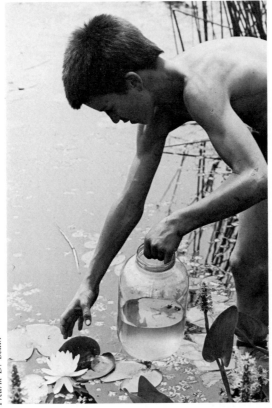

Fredrik D. Bodin

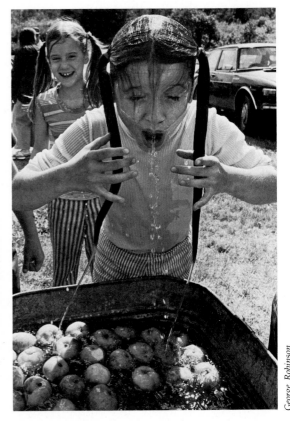

George Robinson

Take a moment to think ahead and adjust the camera's controls to advantage while children are engrossed in some activity. If you expect a subject to move fast (as in the pictures this page), set your shutter to a fast speed if you want action to be sharp in the photograph. If action is slower or if the subject pauses from time to time, you can use a slower shutter speed and still get a sharp picture.

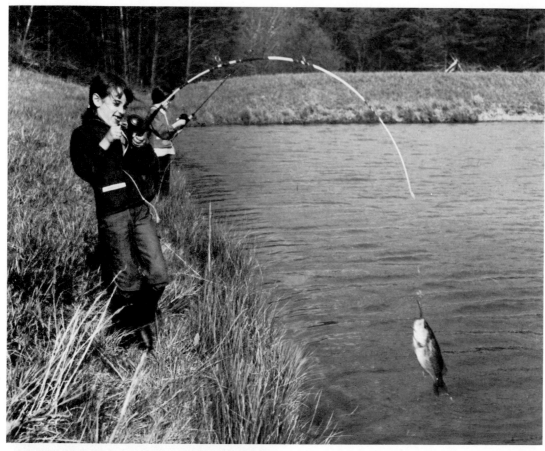

Ronald Parson, Jr.

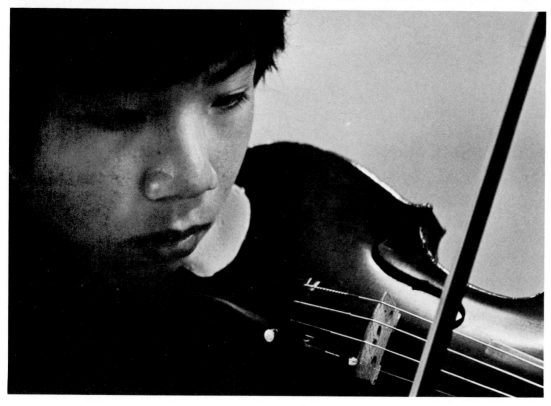

Fredrik D. Bodin

AN ENVIRONMENTAL PORTRAIT

People shape the space around them, and photographing them in their own environment—where they live or work or wherever they have established a corner of their own—can tell much more about them than just a straight head-and-shoulders portrait. How the subject sits or stands—quietly on her porch or tense with the effort of a power lift—adds an extra dimension to his or her character and to the portrait.

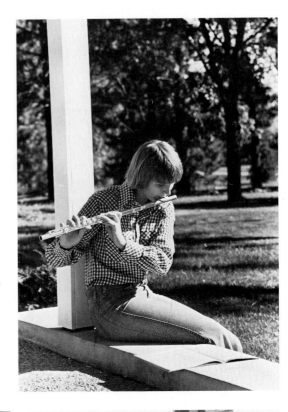

A flute player seems completely at ease and relaxed as she practices on her porch. Sunshine, grass, and trees add a pleasant, peaceful note.

A power lifter focuses all her attention on her lift and dominates the attention of everyone else in the room as well.

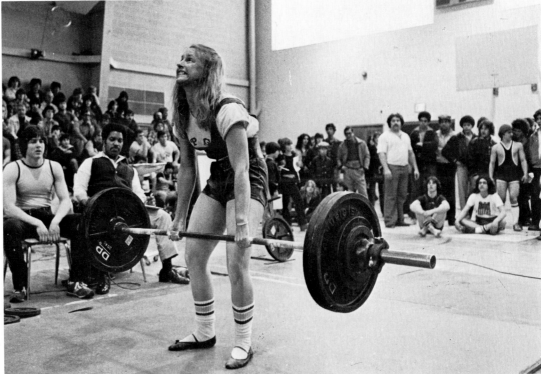

Ken Robert Buck

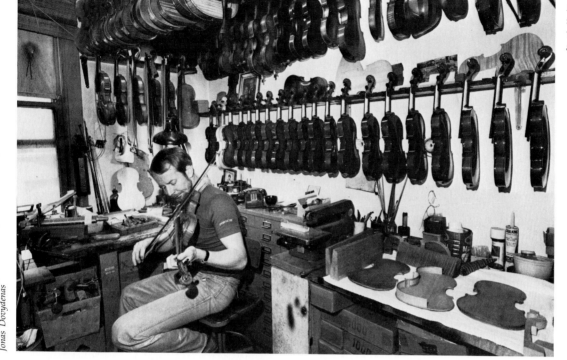

A violin maker has surrounded himself with his product in addition to his tools.

Jonas Dovydenas

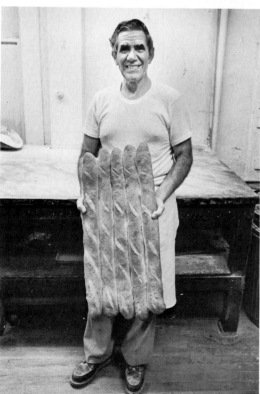

Jonas Dovydenas

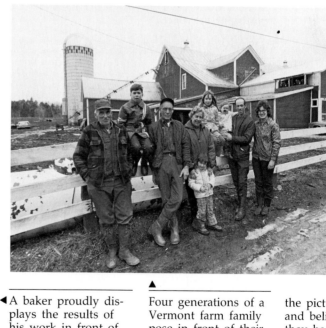

Byron Schumaker

◄ A baker proudly displays the results of his work in front of the table on which he had kneaded and shaped the loaves a short time earlier.

▲ Four generations of a Vermont farm family pose in front of their dairy operation. Their work clothes make the picture realistic and believable, as if they had just stepped away from their chores.

PHOTOGRAPHING THE LANDSCAPE/CITYSCAPE

How do you photograph a place?
There are as many different ways to view a scene as there are photographers. Most important for you: What do you want to remember? What is the best part of the place for you? Do you want many buildings from a distance or just one structure up close? Is it the landscape as a whole that is interesting or some particular part of it, like the fences, opposite? How does a place speak to you?

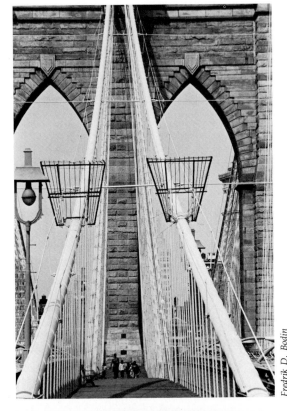

Fredrik D. Bodin

After photographing a standard view of New York City as seen from Brooklyn, across the East River (below), the photographer turned his attention to the nearby Brooklyn Bridge, whose pattern of stone arches and cables creates shapes reminiscent of a Gothic cathedral (right).

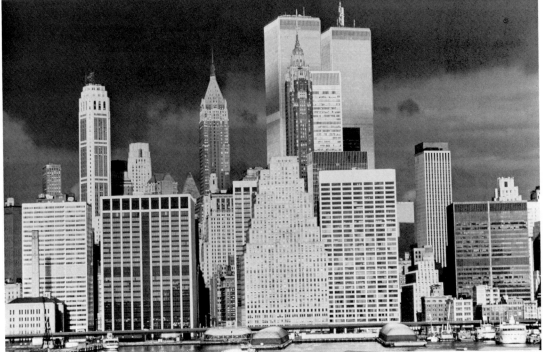

Fredrik D. Bodin

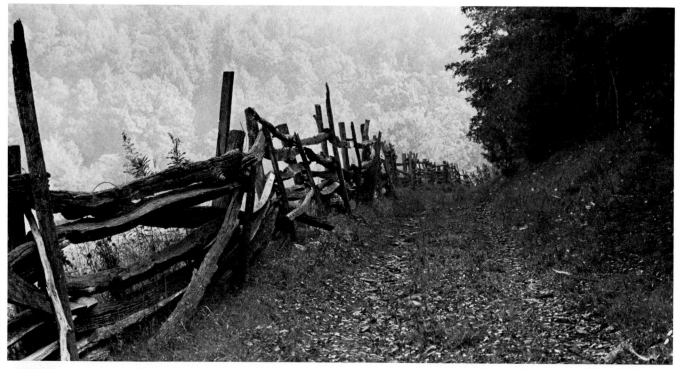

Thomas A. Adler

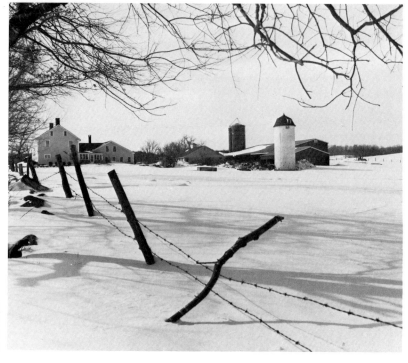

A. L. Weeks

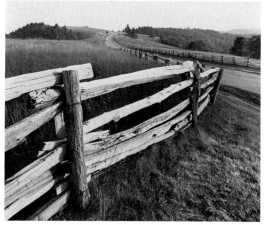

Lyntha Eiler

Landscapes are not always ready-made for the photographer, with dramatic mountains or stormy skies to add interest. Even so, a scene that at first may seem rather ordinary can make an appealing picture if you stop for a moment and look at what is actually present. Here, fences not only draw the eye of the viewer into the scene, but have interesting shapes of their own.

GUIDE TO NIKON
EQUIPMENT AND ACCESSORIES

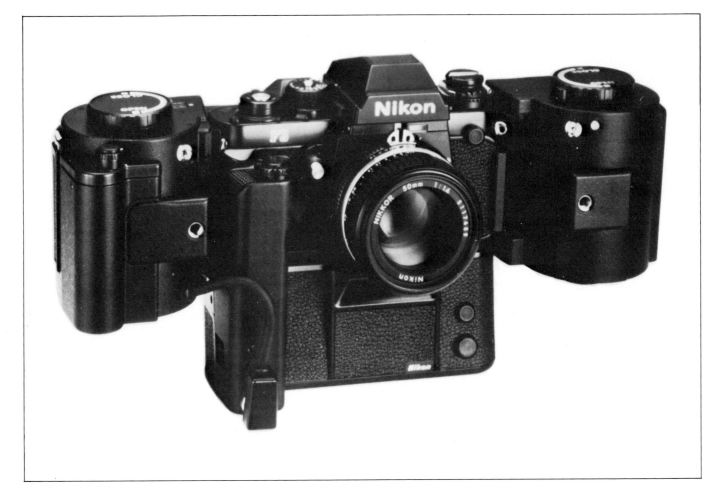

This section prepared by Lista Duren

NIKON CAMERAS: THE FG

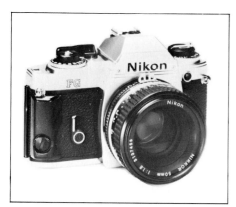

The FG camera is a lightweight, compact model that features programmed automatic exposure, aperture-priority automatic exposure, and manual control. With the SB-15 electronic flash unit, the camera will provide through-the-lens metered automatic flash. The FG also accepts data back and motor drive accessories.

Metering The FG has a center-weighted metering system with a silicon photo diode (SPD) cell that provides fast and accurate metering even in dim light. The meter is activated when the shutter release button is depressed halfway, and it shuts off automatically 16 seconds after you release the button.

Programmed automatic exposure In the programmed mode, the camera sets the exposure controls using a microcomputer to choose an optimum combination of f-stop and shutter speed. This complete automation is useful in situations when the light is changing rapidly and in photojournalism and action photography, when you need to be able to focus and shoot without worrying about camera settings.

Aperture-priority automatic exposure When set on A, the camera will choose the correct shutter speed for the aperture you set, and a viewfinder signal will warn you if the scene being metered is beyond the shutter speed capability for the aperture selected. With this type of automatic exposure you have control over how your pictures will look: you can control depth of field by your choice of aperture, or you can choose to stop or blur action by changing the aperture until the camera selects the shutter speed you want.

Manual exposure You can set both controls yourself with the camera in the manual mode. The viewfinder display will indicate both the shutter speed you have set and the shutter speed recommended by the FG's microcomputer. Manual operation enables you to work creatively with lighting and exposure and to use specialized lenses and close-up accessories that don't couple with the automatic exposure system.

Exposure compensation An unusually light or dark background, such as snow or a heavily shadowed area, can fool the camera's meter into under- or overexposing the main subject. When photographing in such situations, you can use the exposure compensation dial to vary exposure in ½-stop increments up to 2 stops in either direction. The FG also has a backlight button that increases exposure by 2 stops if it is held down when the shutter is released. These controls operate when the camera is in manual or automatic mode.

Shutter The FG has an electronically controlled, vertical-run, metal focal plane shutter that operates at speeds from 1 sec. to 1/1000 sec. Speeds are stepless in the programmed and automatic modes. The B setting for longer exposures is operable with the camera on manual. When the batteries fail, the shutter will operate mechanically at 1/90 sec. and B.

Flash hot shoe The bracket on the pentaprism accepts standard flash units, and for units that are wired for hot-shoe use, it also provides cordless connection to the shutter.

Flash Any of the flash units shown on pages 128–129 will activate the flash-ready light in the viewfinder. The same units will automatically set the shutter to the normal flash sync speed, 1/90 sec. However, in manual mode the shutter speed can be set instead to 1/60 or slower for special effects.

With the Speedlight SB-15 flash, the FG will provide automatic through-the-lens flash metering: the camera will measure the light coming through the lens and cut the flash off at the correct flash exposure even when you have a filter or lens extension device on the camera.

Batteries The FG will accept a 3V lithium battery, two 1.55V silver oxide batteries, or two 1.5V alkaline-manganese batteries. As a battery check, when the batteries are weak, the viewfinder display will turn itself off as soon as the shutter button is released rather than staying lit for 16 seconds as it normally does.

Size, weight, and finish The compact FG body weighs 17.2 oz. (490 g) without a lens. It comes with a detachable hand grip on the front of the camera and is available with chrome or black finish.

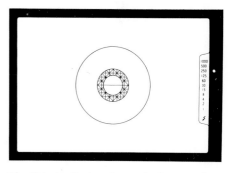

The FG viewfinder shows shutter speeds from 1 to 1/1000 sec. Red LEDs light up to indicate the speed that is set. In manual mode, a blinking LED indicates the suggested speed. Triangular LEDs at the top and bottom of the scale warn of over- and underexposure. The same triangular LEDs blink in the programmed mode if you have not set the lens to the minimum aperture. A thunderbolt-shaped LED functions as the flash-ready light and blinks to warn of underexposure with the SB-15 flash. Additional LEDs tell you when the camera is set for manual operation and warn of lighting conditions beyond the range of the camera's meter.

An audible SONIC (Sound and Optical Nikon Indicator Circuits) warning system may be turned on to warn you of slow shutter speeds and situations that are beyond the camera's metering range.

(Continued on next page)

NIKON CAMERAS: THE FE/THE FE2

(The FG, continued)

Accessories The FG can be used with the MD-E Motor Drive (p. 120), MD-14 Motor Drive (below), and the MF-15 Data Back. The SB-15 flash unit provides automatic through-the-lens metering with the FG, and other flashes described on pages 128–129 may be used as well. The camera also accepts general accessories such as lenses and close-up equipment. Nine different screw-in eyepiece correction lenses are available.

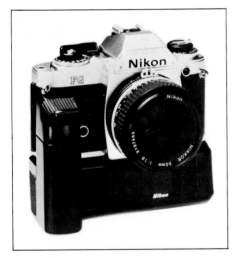

The MD-14 Motor Drive is a lightweight, compact unit designed for the FG and also compatible with the EM camera. It can be used for single-frame shooting or continuous bursts. It features a choice of two shooting speeds: 3.2 frames per second (on "High") or 1.5 frames per second (on "Low"). At the end of the roll of film, the motor automatically shuts off and an LED lights on the motor. The unit is powered by eight 1.5V AA batteries and has a built-in camera grip.

The MF-15 Data Back is interchangeable with the regular back of the FG camera and prints data in the lower right corner of the photograph. The unit has a built-in quartz-controlled clock and a 6-digit liquid crystal display that operates in three modes: date, time, or frame number. With the imprint switch turned on, the back will automatically imprint year/month/day, day/hour/minute, or sequential frame numbers up to 2000. With the switch off, it continues to operate as a digital clock. The unit is powered by two 1.55V silver oxide batteries.

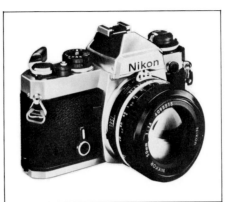

The FE camera is compact and features automatic exposure. Accessories include motor drive, data back, and electronic flash.

Metering Two silicon photo diode (SPD) cells built into the camera measure the light. The system is center-weighted.

Automatic exposure The FE sets exposure automatically in an aperture-priority mode: you select the aperture and the camera meters the light and automatically selects the correct shutter speed. Shutter speeds are stepless, so in addition to the regular settings of 1/250 sec., 1/500 sec., and so on, intermediate speeds such as 1/325 can be utilized.

Automatic exposure compensation For backlit scenes or other special situations you may want to override the camera's automatic controls. The Exposure Compensation Selector lets you do so automatically; in ½-stop increments it will program up to 2 stops increase or decrease of exposure. The FE also has a memory lock that will hold an exposure setting—for example, if you want to move in close to take a reading of a backlit subject.

Manual exposure You can set both aperture and shutter speed yourself if you wish to do so. You can use the camera's meter to determine the exposure by adjusting shutter speed and aperture until two needles visible in the viewfinder are matched.

Shutter Speeds from 1/1000 sec. to 8 sec. (plus B for longer exposures) are available. The all-metal shutter, electronically controlled, travels upward and has a special braking system for quiet, smooth operation.

Flash hot shoe Same as the FG.

Batteries The exposure meter and shutter are powered by two 1.5V silver oxide batteries. A light-emitting diode (LED) battery tester is built in, but even if the batteries are exhausted the shutter continues to operate mechanically at 1/90 sec. and at the B setting.

Size and weight A compact, lightweight camera, the body weighs 20.8 oz. (590 g).

Finish Available in chrome-and-black or all-black finish.

Other features A depth-of-field preview button allows you to stop the lens down to the selected aperture to check depth of field. With the multiple exposure control, you can intentionally expose the same frame more than once. The FE has safeguards against accidental double exposures.

Accessories The FE can be used with the MD-12 Motor Drive for motorized film advance. The SB-10 and SB-E electronic flash units are specially designed for use with the FE. Three types of focusing screens are available—Types K, B, and E (see page 125). The camera accepts all general accessories such as lenses, close-up equipment, and eyepiece accessories. It accepts the Data Back MF-12 shown on page 119.

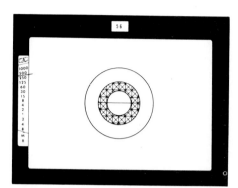

The **FE viewfinder** shows the aperture selected (at top) and a full shutter speed scale (at left). In automatic operation, shown here, a needle indicates the shutter speed selected by the camera's exposure system. In manual match-needle operation, the correct exposure is determined by lining up the shutter speed needle with a second needle. An LED ready light is activated by the SB-E or SB-10 flash unit.

Motor Drive MD-12 (not shown) is a compact, easy-to-attach unit that makes motorized shooting and even remote-control photography possible with the FE, FE2, FM, or FM2 camera. The drive unit attaches directly to the base of the camera. The unit has an anatomical grip with built-in shutter release button; it exposes and advances the film for the next exposure either 1 frame at a time or at rates up to 3.5 frames per second. The unit is powered by eight 1.5V AA alkaline batteries, enough for about 100 rolls of 36-exposure film.

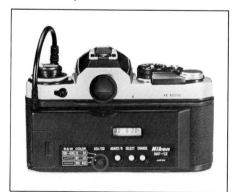

Data Back MF-12 is interchangeable with the regular camera back of the FE, FM, or FM2. During the exposure it imprints the date (year/month/day) or the time (day/hour/minute) or any number from 0 to 99 in the lower right corner of the frame. A liquid crystal display (LCD) on the unit shows the data to be imprinted.

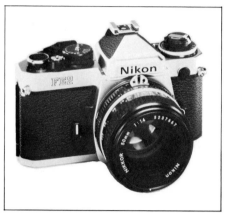

The FE2 is a compact camera with aperture-priority automatic exposure and manual exposure modes. It has all the features of the FE plus an extremely fast titanium shutter and through-the-lens automatic flash exposure control.

Shutter The vertical-travel lightweight titanium shutter provides a shutter speed range of 8 sec. to 1/4000 sec. The flash synchronization speed of 1/250 sec. is fast and well suited for using flash outdoors as fill-in light in bright sunlight.

Flash The camera's through-the-lens light sensing system reads light from the film plane and controls the output of the flash when used with the SB-15 or SB-16 Speedlight. With these units you can set the camera on any f-stop from f/2 to f/22. Other automatic flash units listed on page 129 will provide automatic flash exposure at certain apertures.

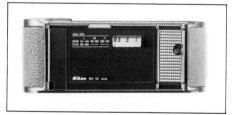

The MF-16 Data Back replaces the back on the FE2 or FM2 cameras and imprints data on the lower right corner of each photograph. The 6-digit liquid crystal display can be set to print year/month/day, day/hour/minute, or frame number up to 2000. An off-on switch gives you the option of printing or not printing data on the film. The back also contains a built-in quartz-controlled clock with an audible alarm signal.

Accessories The FE2 will accept the MF-16 quartz timed data back and the MD-12 motor drive as well as all general accessories.

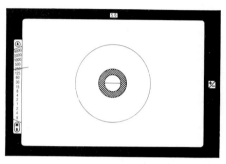

The FE2 viewfinder shows the shutter speed on the left and has readout of the aperture from the lens barrel at the top. In the manual mode, exposure is correct when the black meter needle (which moves as you change the f-stop) matches up with the green needle (which indicates the shutter speed). With the camera in the automatic mode, the green needle moves to A and the black needle indicates the shutter speed setting chosen by the camera. The +/− indicator on the right side lights up when exposure compensation is in effect.

The standard focusing screen is the K2, which has a split-image focusing spot surrounded by a microprism ring. It is about 1 stop brighter than ordinary screens to make focusing easier, especially in dim light. Two other bright screens are available for the FE2. They are the B2 screen for close-ups or with a long telephoto lens, and the E2 which has a grid for architectural work.

NIKON CAMERAS: THE EM/ THE FM/THE FM2

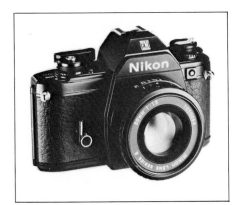

The EM camera is the most compact and economical camera in the Nikon line. It is designed for amateurs who want an automatic camera at a comparatively low cost.

Metering The built-in meter uses a silicon photo diode (SPD) cell. The meter is activated by pressing the shutter release button halfway down; to prevent running down the batteries it shuts itself off automatically about 20 seconds after you release the shutter button.

Operating mode selection Three modes of operation can be selected by turning a dial on top of the camera. "Auto" sets the camera for automatic operation. "M90" provides a mechanical shutter speed of 1/90 sec. and is used for flash units other than the automatically functioning SB-E and SB-10 units. "B" is for long time exposures; the shutter stays open as long as the shutter release button is held down. The camera does not have a fully manual mode in which you can set any combination of shutter speed and aperture yourself.

Automatic exposure The EM has an aperture-priority system: you set the aperture and the camera meters the light and selects the correct shutter speed for normal lighting situations.

Automatic exposure compensation A backlight button, which you can use when the background is much brighter than the subject, automatically increases the exposure about 2 stops so that the subject will not be underexposed.

Shutter In automatic mode the shutter operates at speeds from 1 sec. to 1/1000 sec. Speeds are stepless, which allows the camera to choose speeds between conventional settings for exact exposure control. The vertical-run metal shutter operates electronically at the automatic setting and mechanically at the M90 and B settings.

Flash hot shoe Same as the FG.

Batteries Two 1.5V silver oxide batteries power the shutter and the metering system. The camera has a built-in LED battery check and an automatic meter shutoff to prevent battery drain. When the batteries are exhausted the camera will not function automatically, but the shutter will operate mechanically at two settings, 1/90 sec. and B.

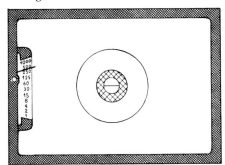

The EM viewfinder shows shutter speeds (at left) with a needle to indicate which speed the camera is using. A red zone at the bottom of the shutter speed scale indicates speeds lower than 1/30 sec. (too slow to hand hold the camera), and another red zone at the top indicates conditions too bright for the camera's fastest exposure. If you don't notice when the needle enters one of the red zones, the camera's SONIC (Sound and Optical Nikon Indicator Circuits) system will beep, reminding you to try a different aperture.

With the SB-E or SB-10 flash, an LED signal in the viewfinder lights up when the flash is ready to fire. In addition, with the SB-E the signal blinks if the camera is not properly set.

Size, weight, and finish The smallest camera in the Nikon system, the EM measures only 5⁹/₁₆ × 3⅜ × 2⅛ in. (134.5 × 85.9 × 54 mm); the body weighs 16 oz. (460 g). It comes with a black finish.

Accessories The EM accepts accessories such as the SB-E and SB-10 electronic flash units (see page 128), MD-E Motor Drive, Nikkor AI and Nikon Series E lenses. All Nikkor lenses, close-up attachments, and other front-end accessories that fit Nikon cameras can be used with the EM.

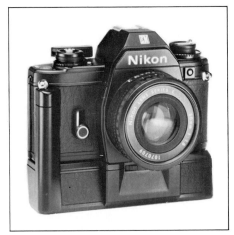

The MD-E Motor Drive is a lightweight unit made for the EM camera and also compatible with the FG. With the MD-E, pressing the camera's shutter release button exposes the film and automatically advances it to the next frame. Exposures can be made a single frame at a time or the unit can be set for continuous firing at rates up to 2 frames per second.

An LED signal flashes each time the film is advanced and stays lit at the end of the roll when the motor automatically stops. The unit is powered by six 1.5V AAA penlight batteries, enough for about fifty rolls of 36-exposure film. The unit has a built-in grip and a tripod socket. It attaches easily to the camera with a thumbscrew and does not have to be removed when you change film.

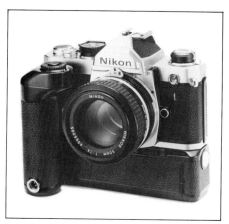

The FM camera is compact and lightweight with manually operated exposure controls. Its accessories include motor drive, flash, and a data back.

Metering Two gallium photo diode cells meter light through the lens, responding instantly to changes in light level, even in dim light. The metering system is center-weighted.

Exposure For all normal situations the lens aperture or shutter speed control or both are adjusted until a light-emitting diode (LED) display in the camera's viewfinder signals that the exposure is correct.

Shutter Speeds from 1/1000 sec. to 1 sec. (plus B for longer exposures) are provided by the all-metal, vertical-run shutter.

Flash hot shoe Same as the FG.

Batteries Two 1.5V silver oxide batteries power the exposure meter, and a battery check is provided to test the strength of the batteries. Only the meter becomes inoperative if the batteries are exhausted; the camera continues to function in every other way.

Size and weight Compact and lightweight, the body weighs 20.8 oz. (590 g). Full-sized controls are designed for fast, comfortable handling.

Finish Available in chrome-and-black or all-black finish.

Other features The depth-of-field preview lever stops the lens down to the selected aperture so that you can check depth of field. A multiple exposure button on the top of the camera lets you make multiple exposures whenever you want to.

Accessories The FM accepts the Motor Drive MD-12 (page 119) and Data Back MF-12 (page 117), as well as flash units, lenses, close-up equipment, and all general accessories.

The FM viewfinder provides full exposure ▶ information: aperture (top) and shutter speed (left). Three LEDs light up to indicate underexposure, correct exposure, and overexposure in five possible combinations (see below). The camera is equipped with a Type K focusing screen which has a split-image spot surrounded by a microprism collar on a matte field.

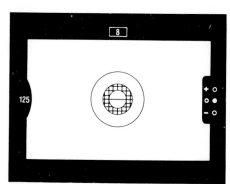

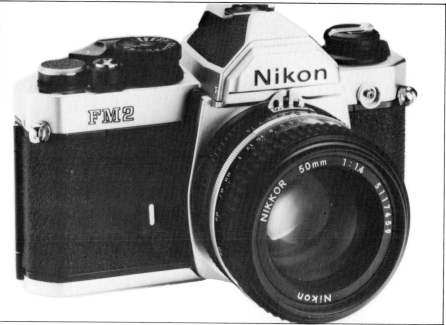

The FM2 camera is a manual model with all the features of the FM. In addition the FM2 offers extra fast shutter speeds, flash sync speeds up to 1/200 sec., and interchangeable focusing screens.

Shutter The new specially treated titanium shutter is extremely strong and rigid, so it can withstand a higher spring tension than conventional shutters and deliver faster shutter speeds. The resulting shutter speed range is 1/4000 sec. to 1 sec. (plus B for longer exposures). All shutter speeds are mechanical; they do not rely on batteries.

Flash The hot-shoe bracket on the pentaprism automatically connects Nikon flash models SB-10, SB-15, or SB-E to the camera's shutter and to the ready/warning light in the viewfinder. Other flash units, including the Nikon SB-11 and SB-14, require a connecting cord for synchronization. Shutter speeds of 1/200 sec. or slower may be used with flash.

Accessories Accessories include the Motor Drive MD-12, the Data Back MF-12 or MF-16, lenses, flash units, close-up equipment, and general accessories.

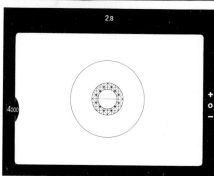

The FM2 viewfinder tells you the shutter speed (left) and the aperture (top) that are set on the camera. Three LEDs on the right light up in five different configurations to indicate correct exposure, overexposure, and/ underexposure. The FM2 comes with a Type K screen which has a split-image rangefinder in the center surrounded by a microprism collar. The rest of the screen is matte-surfaced. The focusing screen is interchangeable with Type B or Type E screens (see page 125). Screens are easy to change yourself with a special tweezer tool that comes with the camera.

NIKON CAMERAS: THE F3 SERIES

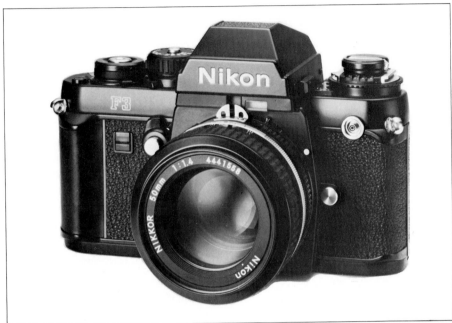

The F3, like Nikon's previous F series 35mm cameras, is a favorite of professionals for its versatility, precision, and ruggedness. Lenses, viewfinders, and focusing screens are readily interchangeable. Flash, motor drive, and other accessories make the F3 a flexible tool for any assignment—professional or personal.

Automatic exposure An aperture-priority camera: you set the aperture and the camera automatically selects the correct stepless shutter speed for normal exposure.

Automatic exposure override For back-lit scenes or for special effects, the automatic exposure can be increased or decreased by as much as 2 stops in 1/3-stop increments. An exposure memory lock holds a given reading—for example, if you want to meter a subject up close then step back to take the picture.

Metered manual exposure You adjust aperture, shutter speed, or both. The camera's built-in meter can be used to set camera controls.

Metering The F3's behind-the-mirror metering system lets light pass through the lens and then through microscopic holes in the reflex mirror. The light

strikes a secondary mirror that reflects the light to a silicon photo diode (SPD) cell for the exposure reading. The system is center weighted, with about 80% of its sensitivity concentrated in a central 12mm area of the observed scene.

Viewfinders The F3 has five interchangeable viewfinders, each with full metering and exposure display (see details, pages 124–125). They are easy to change—they simply snap into place on the camera body.

Focusing screens fit beneath the viewfinder and are also interchangeable. Twenty screens are available (see page 125).

Shutter The F3's extremely strong quilted titanium foil shutter is exceptionally accurate and resistant to heat, humidity, and long, hard use. Speeds range from 8 sec. to 1/2000 sec. "B" and "T" settings are available for long exposures.

Flash units SB-11, SB-12, and SB-14 can integrate with the F3 camera's through-the-lens exposure control system, which measures the light during the exposure and terminates the flash when exposure is complete. More about these and other Nikon flash units on pages 128–129.

Batteries Two 1.5V silver oxide batteries power the meter, shutter, and finder. Mechanical settings at 1/60 sec. and T permit shutter operation if batteries fail.

Size, weight, and finish The F3 body without lens measures 5.85 × 3.8 × 2.58 in. (148.5 × 96.5 × 65.5 mm) and weighs 24.7 oz. (700 g). Available in professional all-black finish.

Other features The F3 won't allow accidental double exposures, but when you want to expose the same frame more than once, the multiple exposure lever lets you do so. A depth-of-field preview button on the front of the camera lets you stop the lens down to the selected aperture to check depth of field. A mirror lock-up lever allows you to lock the mirror in the up position. It is useful for close-up shooting, motor-drive photography, or with super-telephoto lenses.

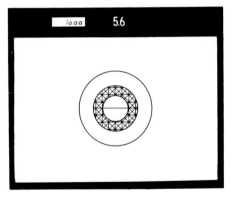

The F3 viewfinder shows both shutter speed and aperture settings. In automatic operation (illustrated here) the shutter speed closest to the operative speed appears in a liquid crystal display (LCD). Under- or overexposure is signaled if the selected aperture cannot be matched to a suitable shutter speed. The selected aperture appears in the aperture direct readout (ADR) window.

In manual operation, shutter speed and aperture are displayed, along with + and – symbols used to determine correct exposure. With compatible flash units such as the SB-12, a flash-ready light indicates when the unit has fully recycled and is ready to fire. The light also signals if flash mounting or flash exposure is not correct.

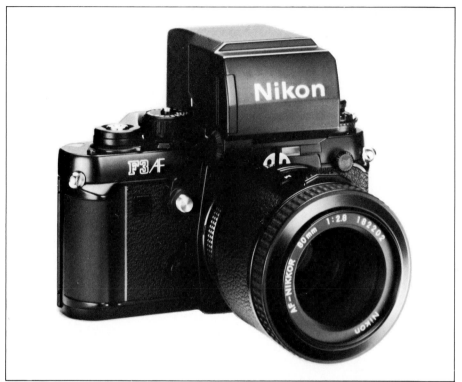

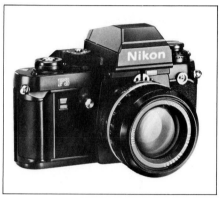

Autofocus lenses The AF Nikkor 80mm f/2.8 and the AF Nikkor 200mm f/3.5 provide automatic focusing at two of the focal lengths most often used in sports and action photography. Both lenses have a switch for manual or automatic operation and a focus-lock button so that the scene can be focused and then recomposed off-center. For more about auto-focus lenses, see page 126.

The F3HP camera is identical to the F3 in every respect except that it comes with the High Eyepoint Finder DE-3 (described on page 124), which is designed for photographers who wear glasses or goggles.

The F3/T camera (not shown) has all the features of the F3 plus an extra-rugged body strengthened with titanium. The standard viewfinder for the F3/T is the titanium-covered DE-4 High Eyepoint Finder, designed for photographers wearing glasses or goggles. The F3/T is available in chrome finish and the body weighs 26 oz. (740 g).

The F3AF features the same exposure and metering systems as the F3. In addition, this camera will provide fully automatic focusing with AF Nikkor lenses and focusing guidance with most Nikkor and Series E lenses of f/3.5 or faster.

The AF Finder DX-1 contains two optical SPD (silicon photo diode) sensors that electronically detect focus shift and activate micromotors which bring the camera's AF lens into focus. With the AF lens set on manual or with a non-AF lens on the camera, the finder will provide focusing assistance with red LEDs in the viewfinder display. The AF Finder DX-1 will also provide focusing guidance when used on other F3-series cameras.

Accessories The MK-1 Firing Rate Converter makes it possible to use the MD-4 Motor Drive (shown on page 124) for autofocused pictures at speeds of 1, 2, or 3 frames per second. The SB-16A and SB-12 Speedlight flash units provide through-the-lens automatic flash exposure with the F3AF. The SB-11 and SB-14 Speedlights will do the same with an SC-12 TTL Sensor Cord.

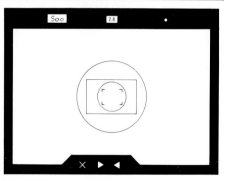

The F3AF viewfinder shows the shutter speed and the aperture at the top and has a flash-ready light as in the F3 viewfinder. Red arrows at the bottom tell you which way to turn the lens for correct focus. Both arrows light up when the scene is in focus. A red X lights up when subject contrast or brightness is insufficient for automatic focusing. The focusing indicators also function as a battery check.

Brackets in the center of the frame mark the area that is read by the autofocus sensors. The subject must be composed within this area. Then, by locking in the focus, you can recompose the scene with the subject off-center.

The noninterchangeable focusing screen has a matte fresnel field with a clear center area.

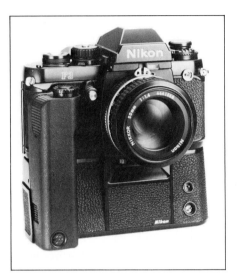

Motor drive with the F3 automatically exposes and advances the film and cocks the shutter for the next exposure, either a single frame at a time or firing continuously at rates up to 6 frames per second. Motor drive has become standard equipment for photojournalists and is useful for anyone who wants fast or uninterrupted camera action.

The MD-4 Motor Drive (shown here) attaches to the baseplate of the F3 camera. The hand grip contains a shutter button and a selector for single-frame or continuous operation. Film rewind is also motorized.

Motor drive accessories for the MD-4 include nickel-cadmium or alkaline battery holders, an AC/DC power converter, an intervalometer that automatically triggers the camera at preset intervals, as in time-lapse photography, and devices to trigger the camera by remote control.

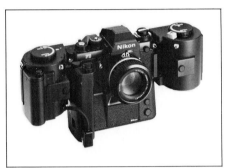

A 250-exposure back allows you to load the camera with a roll of film up to 250 frames long. This is especially useful for uninterrupted shooting of fast-moving events, or for remote control photography. The MF-4 250-exposure back, designed for use with the F3 camera and MD-4 Motor Drive, has additive and subtractive frame counters and a built-in micromotor to drive the take-up magazine.

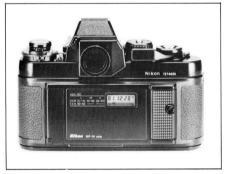

The MF-14 Data Back is an accessory back for the F3 camera that imprints data in the lower right corner of each photograph. A built-in quartz-controlled clock, which is programmed until February, 2100, provides a digital readout on a six-digit liquid-crystal-display panel. The data back can be used to imprint year/month/day, day/hour/minute, or sequential frame numbering up to 2000. The imprint switch can be turned off when you don't want to record data on the film. The back functions as a digital clock even when you aren't using it to imprint the film, and it includes an audible alarm signal. It is powered by two 1.55V silver oxide batteries.

F3 viewing options include five interchangeable viewfinders (described below) and twenty easy-to-insert focusing screens (illustrated on page 125). No exposure compensation is required for any combination of finder and screen.

Interchangeable viewfinders The F3 gives you your choice of five viewfinders, each of which retains full metering capability plus liquid crystal display (LCD) for exposure information.

Pentaprism DE-2 is supplied as standard equipment with the F3. The image is viewed at eye level and is exceptionally bright and clear. The large eyepiece makes it easy to view the entire scene even if you are wearing eyeglasses. The finder accepts eyepiece correction lenses (see page 132) and has a built-in eyepiece shutter, useful for automatic remote photography.

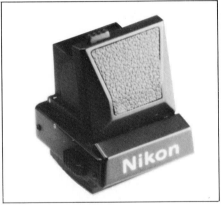

Waist-Level Finder DW-3 is designed for close-up or copy photography or for using the camera at a low level or over your head. You view the image by looking into the top of the camera instead of by looking straight ahead. The finder has a built-in 5X magnifier that flips up for critical focusing. The top of the finder folds flat when not in use.

High Eyepoint Finder DE-3 is an eye-level viewfinder that enables people who wear glasses to see the entire frame including exposure information with the eye up to 1 inch (25 mm) away from the eyepiece. It is designed for people who wear glasses or goggles and it also makes faster framing possible if you don't wear glasses. The Eyepiece Adapter DK-1 makes it possible to attach the Right Angle Viewing Attachment DR-3, the Eyepiece Magnifier DG-2, or an eyepiece correction lens (all described on page 132) to the Finder DE-3.

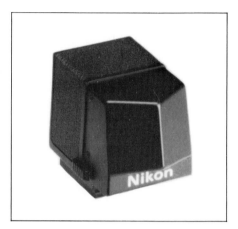

Action Finder DA-2 has an extra-large eyepiece that permits full viewing and focusing when the eye is as far as 2.4 in. (60 mm) from the eyepiece. This is useful for following action in sports photography and is ideal when the camera is in an underwater housing or must be used with goggles.

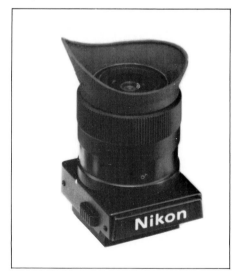

6X Focusing Finder DW-4 magnifies the entire viewfinder image six times and is helpful in macrophotography, astrophotography, or other work when critical focusing is essential. It can be used with Type C or M focusing screens for aerial (parallax) focusing. The finder comes with a rubber eyecup and doubles as a loupe for magnifying and examining slides.

Focusing screens The Type K screen supplied as standard equipment on Nikon cameras is the most popular one for general photography, but other types of screens may be better in certain situations or a photographer may have an individual preference. Any of the screens shown can be used with the F3 camera. Types K, B, and E are also interchangeable on the FE and FM2 cameras. Screens K2, B2, and E2, which are extra-bright versions of the K, B, and E screens, are available for the FE2 camera. All the screens except Types C, D, H, M, and R have a 12mm central circle that outlines the area read by Nikon's center-weighted exposure meter system.

Type A Matte/fresnel field with split-image rangefinder spot. For use with lenses of up to 400mm focal length, f/4.5 or faster.

Type B Matte/fresnel with ground-glass center. For long-focal-length lenses and small maximum apertures (f/5.6 to f/11).

Type C Fine-ground matte with central clear spot and cross-hair reticle. For photomicrography and other work involving high magnification.

Type D All matte, fine-ground. For long-focal-length lenses.

Type E Matte/fresnel with fine-ground matte spot, multiple horizontal and vertical lines. For architectural or other work requiring exact alignment.

Type G series Clear fresnel with central microprism spot. Provides brilliant image for use in dim light. Available in four models to match specific lenses.

Type H series Clear fresnel with microprism pattern over whole area. Provides optimum edge-to-edge brightness for use in dim light. Available in four models to match specific lenses.

Type J Matte/fresnel with microprism spot. For general use.

Type K Matte/fresnel with split-image rangefinder spot surrounded by microprism ring. For general use.

Type L Similar to Type A but with split-image spot at 45° angle. Facilitates focusing on horizontal lines.

Type M Clear with double cross-hair reticle and scales in 1mm increments. For high-magnification work.

Type P Matte/fresnel with split-image spot at angle plus microprism ring and vertical and horizontal lines.

Type R Combines features of Types A and E.

TV-format screen Matte/fresnel with central split-image spot. Engraved lines show standard TV frame plus "safe" areas for recording action and titles.

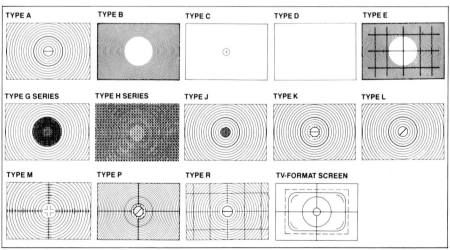

NIKKOR AND NIKON LENSES

Nikkor lenses, some of which are shown below, offer outstanding creative possibilities: a 2000mm super-telephoto can make close-ups of subjects so far away that they are invisible or barely visible to the unaided eye; a 6mm fisheye has an angle of view so wide (220°) that it actually records objects slightly behind itself; and more than sixty other lenses with different focal lengths in between are also available.

Optical performance of Nikkor lenses is renowned. Each lens receives Nikon's multilayer integrated coating (NIC), which significantly reduces internal reflections to improve image contrast and color fidelity. Many Nikkor wide-angle lenses have a "floating element" system that repositions some lens elements automatically as the focusing ring is turned; this system prevents the optical distortions that occur at the close focusing distances often used with wide-angle lenses and so produces excellent performance over the entire focusing range. An internal focusing (IF) design improves the performance of several Nikkor telephoto lenses as well as appreciably reducing their length.

AI (Automatic Indexing) lenses simplify lens interchange and use. An AI lens automatically programs the camera's exposure meter for metering at the widest lens aperture, so that the viewfinder image is always at its brightest even during metering. Some Nikkor lenses do not incorporate the AI feature, so meter readings are made with the lens stopped down to the taking aperture. When an AI lens is used with an FE, FM, FM2, or F3 camera, the aperture in use is shown in the camera's viewfinder via a direct readout from a secondary aperture scale at the rear of the lens (Aperture Direct Reading, or ADR). Most older Nikkor lenses that have a meter-coupling shoe and an automatic diaphragm can be converted to AI/ADR operation.

Nikon Series E lenses are compact, lightweight, and economical, and are specially designed for compact cameras such as the EM (the 50mm f/1.8 Series E lens is shown mounted on the EM camera on page 120).

Nikkor autofocus lenses, when used with the F3AF camera body and the AF Finder DX-1, can automatically bring a scene into sharp focus in a fraction of a second. The standard bayonet mount has AF contacts which relay focusing signals and battery power from the camera body to micromotors in the lens. Focus-lock buttons enable you to lock in the focus on a centered subject and then move off-center for the exposure. The 200mm AF lens has four distance range settings so that you can track action (when photographing sports, for example) without interference from nearer or farther subjects. Autofocus lenses can also be used for regular manual focusing. For more about the F3AF camera, see page 123.

Nikon filters are made of the same optical glass used in Nikkor lenses, and each side is precision-ground and polished to be absolutely flat and parallel. Front and back surfaces are optically coated to prevent surface reflections. The filters are made in different sizes to fit the diameters of Nikon lenses. Information about the effects of various filters on color and black-and-white film appears on pages 74–75.

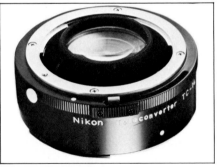

A teleconverter is an accessory lens that is placed between camera and lens to increase focal length. This TC-14 Teleconverter increases lens focal length 1.4X when used with any AI-Nikkor lens from 300 mm through 1200 mm. (For example, a 1200 mm lens plus the TC-14 Teleconverter has an effective focal length of 1680 mm.) The TC-200 Teleconverter (not shown) doubles the focal length of any lens up to 200 mm in focal length; the TC-300 doubles the focal length of most lenses 300 mm or longer.

Nikon Series E lenses technical specifications

Focal length	Aperture range	Diaphragm	Angle of view	Filter size
28mm AI	f/2.8–f/22	Auto	74°	52mm
35mm AI	f/2.5–f/22	Auto	62°	52mm
50mm AI	f/1.8–f/22	Auto	46°	52mm
100mm AI	f/2.8–f/22	Auto	24°20'	52mm
135mm AI	f/2.8–f/32	Auto	18°	52mm
36–72mm AI	f/3.5–f/22	Auto	62°–33°30'	52mm
75–150mm AI	f/3.5–f/32	Auto	31°40'–17°	52mm
70–210mm AI	f/4–f/32	Auto	34°20'–11°50'	62mm

Nikkor autofocus lenses technical specifications

Focal length	Aperture range	Diaphragm	Angle of view	Filter size
80mm	f/2.8–f/32	Auto	30°20'	52mm
200mm	f/3.5–f/32	Auto	12°20'	62mm

Nikkor lenses technical specifications

	Focal length	Aperture range	Diaphragm	Angle of view	Filter size
Fisheye Nikkor lenses	6mm AI	f/2.8–f/22	Auto	220°	Built-in
	8mm AI	f/2.8–f/22	Auto	180°	Built-in
	16mm AI	f/2.8–f/22	Auto	180°	Supplied
Wide-angle Nikkor lenses	13mm AI	f/5.6–f/22	Auto	118°	Behind-lens
	15mm AI	f/3.5–f/22	Auto	110°	Supplied
	18mm AI	f/3.5–f/22	Auto	100°	72mm
	20mm AI	f/3.5–f/22	Auto	94°	52mm
	24mm AI	f/2–f/22	Auto	84°	52mm
	24mm AI	f/2.8–f/22	Auto	84°	52mm
	28mm AI	f/2–f/22	Auto	74°	52mm
	28mm AI	f/2.8–f/22	Auto	74°	52mm
	28mm AI	f/3.5–f/22	Auto	74°	52mm
	35mm AI	f/1.4–f/16	Auto	62°	52mm
	35mm AI	f/2–f/22	Auto	62°	52mm
	35mm AI	f/2.8–f/22	Auto	62°	52mm
Normal Nikkor lenses	50mm AI	f/1.2–f/16	Auto	46°	52mm
	50mm AI	f/1.4–f/16	Auto	46°	52mm
	50mm AI	f/1.8–f/22	Auto	46°	52mm
Telephoto Nikkor lenses	85mm AI	f/1.4–f/16	Auto	28°30′	72mm
	85mm AI	f/2–f/22	Auto	28°30′	52mm
	105mm	f/1.8–f/22	Auto	23°20′	62mm
	105mm AI	f/2.5–f/32	Auto	23°20′	52mm
	135mm AI	f/2–f/22	Auto	18°	72mm
	135mm AI	f/2.8–f/32	Auto	18°	52mm
	135mm AI	f/3.5–f/32	Auto	18°	52mm
	180mm ED/AI	f/2.8–f/32	Auto	13°40′	72mm
	200mm AI	f/4–f/32	Auto	12°20′	52mm
	300mm AI	f/4.5–f/22	Auto	8°10′	72mm
ED-Nikkor telephoto lenses (for direct camera mounting)	200mm IF-ED	f/2–f/22	Auto	12°20′	122mm
	300mm IF-ED	f/2–f/16	Auto	8°10′	160mm or 52mm
	300mm IF-ED	f/2.8–f/32	Auto	8°10′	122mm
	300mm IF-ED/AI	f/4.5–f/22	Auto	8°10′	72mm
	400mm IF-ED/AI	f/3.5–f/22	Auto	6°10′	122mm or 39mm R
	400mm IF-ED/AI	f/5.6–f/32	Auto	6°10′	72mm
	600mm IF-ED/AI	f/4–f/22	Auto	4°10′	160mm; also 39mm insertion type
	600mm IF-ED/AI	f/5.6–f/32	Auto	4°10′	122mm or 39mm R
	800mm IF-ED/AI	f/8–f/32	Auto	3°	122mm or 39mm R
	1200mm IF-ED/AI	f/11–f/32	Auto	2°	122mm or 39mm R
Reflex Nikkor lenses	500mm	f/8	Fixed	5°	39mm behind-lens
	1000mm	f/11	Fixed	2°30′	39mm behind-lens
	2000mm	f/11	Fixed	1°10′	Built-in
Zoom Nikkor lenses	25–50mm AI	f/4–f/22	Auto	80°40′–47°50′	72mm
	35–70mm AI	f/3.5–f/22	Auto	62°–34°20′	62mm
	35–105mm	f/3.5–f/22	Auto	62°–23°20′	52mm
	50–135mm	f/3.5–f/22	Auto	46°–18°	62mm
	50–300mm ED/AI	f/4.5–f/22	Auto	46°–8°10′	95mm
	80–200mm	f/2.8–f/32	Auto	30°10′–12°20′	95mm
	80–200mm AI	f/4–f/32	Auto	30°10′–12°20′	62mm
	180–600mm ED/AI	f/8–f/32	Auto*	13°40′–4°10′	95mm
	200–400mm ED	f/4–f/32	Auto	12°–6°	122mm
	200–600mm AI	f/9.5–f/32	Auto*	12°20′–4°10′	Series 9
	360–1200mm ED/AI	f/11–f/32	Auto*	6°50′–2°	122mm
Micro Nikkor lenses and special Nikkor lenses	55mm Micro AI	f/2.8–f/32	Auto	43°	52mm
	105mm Micro AI	f/4–f/32	Auto	23°20′	52mm
	200mm Micro AI	f/4–f/32	Auto	12°20′	52mm
	28mm PC	f/3.5–f/22	Manual	74°	72mm
	35mm PC	f/2.8–f/32	Manual	62°	52mm
	58mm Noct AI	f/1.2–f/16	Auto	40°50′	52mm
	Medical 120mm IF	f/4–f/32	Auto	18°50′ (1/11×)	49mm

ED lenses feature Extra-Low Dispersion optical glass.
IF (Internal Focusing) lenses incorporate internally moving lens groups.
*Stop-down exposure measurement.
R – rear filter.

NIKON ELECTRONIC FLASH UNITS

Nikon flash units feature energy-saving thyristor circuitry. Unused energy is recycled back into the system instead of simply being discharged, resulting in longer battery life and shorter recycling times. Features of Nikon flash units listed in the chart opposite are explained below. More about flash and how to use it appears on pages 90–95.

The guide number for a flash is a measurement of its power. The higher the guide number for a given film speed (ASA), the brighter the flash and the farther you can use it from the subject.

Auto aperture choices Automatic flash units have photo sensor cells that read the light bouncing off the subject and end flash discharge when the exposure is complete. These units are designed to operate automatically only at certain apertures. The wider the choice of apertures, the greater the range of camera-to-

subject distances within which you can use the flash in its automatic mode and the more control you have over depth of field in a particular shot.

Through-the-lens (TTL) automatic flash exposure is controlled by the camera's through-the-lens meter (rather than by a sensor on the flash unit). Any f-stop on the camera lens may be used. Because the light is read at the film plane, the flash exposure will automatically compensate for filters or longer-than-normal lens extensions.

Recycling time is the length of time it takes to recharge the unit for the next flash after a picture has been taken. If you want to take flash shots in quick succession, as with a power winder, you will want a flash unit capable of a short recycling time. Recycling time varies depending on the aperture selected and the type of batteries used.

Angle of coverage Most Nikon flash units illuminate an area as wide as that seen by a 35mm lens, so they can be used with any lens of 35mm or longer focal length. The shorter the focal length of the camera lens, the wider the angle that the flash must illuminate. Many units have a wide-angle diffuser that fits over the light to broaden its coverage.

Bounce capability gives you the option of tilting the head of the flash to bounce light off a ceiling, wall, or reflector. For correct automatic flash exposure, the flash sensor remains pointed straight ahead when the flash head tilts. Some flash heads tilt only in the vertical plane; others turn from side to side as well.

Mount Most flash units slip onto the camera's hot shoe, which holds the flash in place and provides an electronic connection to the camera's exposure system and viewfinder display. Handle-mount flash units are held in place with a bracket and a synch cord provides the electronic connection.

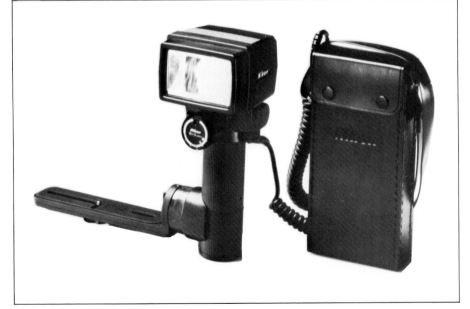

The Speedlight SB-14 electronic flash is a high-powered handle-mount unit with several features that make it suitable for professional use. It provides through-the-lens automatic exposure when connected to the F3 camera with Remote Sensor Cord SC-12. For multiple-flash exposures, the SB-14 has a special slave setting that causes the unit to emit light pulsed at a frequency to trigger other flash units. For bounced light, the flash head rotates and tilts with click stops every 30°.

Power for the SB-14 is supplied by the over-the-shoulder SD-7 battery pack. It holds six C batteries and comes with a power supply cord that plugs into the external power terminal on the flash unit. It will accept rechargeable Ni-Cad batteries, alkaline-manganese batteries, or manganese batteries.

The ML-1 Modulite, a remote triggering device for motorized Nikon cameras, may also be used as a remote receiver to trigger a slave flash. Because the ML-1's sensor responds only to the special pulsed light given off by the SB-11 or SB-14 flash, the slave flash it controls will not go off in response to another photographer's flash.

	SB-10	SB-E	SB-11	SB-12	SB-14	SB-15	SB-16
Guide number for ASA 100 film and distance measured							
in feet	82	56	118	82	105	82	138*
in meters	25	17	36	25	32	25	42
Number of apertures usable with automatic operation	2	3	3	†	3	2	2
Through-the-lens auto exposure possible with			F3 (with SC-12 remote cord)	F3	F3 (with SC-12 remote cord)	FG	F3 series FE2 FG
Recycling time	1–8 sec.	9 sec.	1–8 sec.	1–8 sec.	4–12 sec.	1–8 sec.	8–11 sec.
Coverage	35mm	35mm	35mm	35mm	28mm	35mm	28 mm
with wide-angle adapter	28mm	28mm	28mm	28mm	24mm	28mm	24 mm
Bounce capability	—	—	120° vert.	—	120° vert. 240° horiz.	90° vert.	90° vert. 270° horiz.
Mount	hot shoe	hot shoe	handle mount	hot shoe	handle mount	hot shoe	hot shoe

*Varies with zoom head and mode setting.
†Manual operation only with all cameras except the F3.

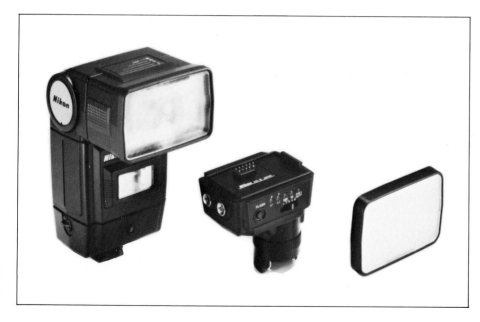

The **Speedlight SB-16** electronic flash features a dual flash head which combines an omnidirectional main zoom head for bounce light and a smaller stationary flash head for fill flash. The flash integrates with the TTL metering system in the F3, FE2, and FG cameras, and provides regular automatic control with other Nikon cameras. The unit also has a manual setting for full flash output at the aperture you select and a motor-drive mode which allows consecutive automatic exposures at speeds up to 4 frames per second for sequences up to 8 frames long. The zoom head may be set to match the angle of view of the lens in use. The unit requires an AS-8 Flash Unit Coupler for use with F3-series cameras, and an AS-9 coupler for use with the FE2 or FG camera. It is shown here with the AS-8 coupler.

NIKON CLOSE-UP EQUIPMENT

Nikon close-up equipment can help you to move in just a little closer to take a picture of a wildflower, to photograph its seeds life-size or larger, or to record a cross-section of its stem through a microscope. Pages 80–83 explain close-up equipment and techniques in more detail.

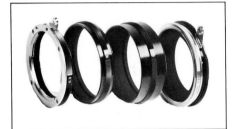

Extension rings fit between the camera and its lens. They give more potential magnification than close-up lens attachments but are still a compact and economical means of producing a close-up. *Extension Ring Set K* (shown here) includes five rings from 5.8 mm to 20 mm in length (total combined length is 46.6 mm) that can be used separately or in combination to produce a variety of magnification with any lens from 18 mm to 300 mm. Metering through the lens is done with the lens stopped down, and the diaphragm is closed manually when an exposure is made. Extension Ring E2 can be added to provide semiautomatic diaphragm operation.

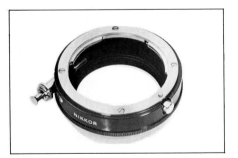

Extension Ring BR-4 (9 mm long) has a push-button control that opens the lens to full aperture for viewing and focusing and closes it to preset the aperture for metering and exposure. A cable release can be attached to operate the control. *Automatic Extension Rings PK-11, 12, and 13 (not shown)* are respectively 8 mm, 14 mm, and 27.5 mm long and provide full-aperture metering and automatic diaphragm control on Nikkor AI and Nikon Series E lenses.

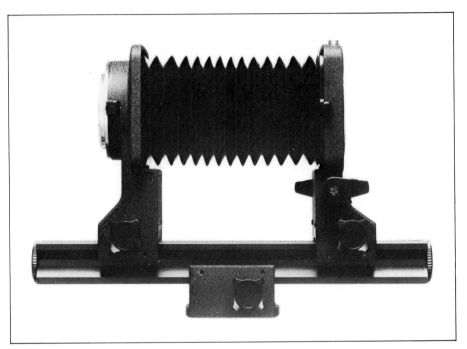

Bellows attachments fit between the camera and the lens and give the greatest flexibility in close-up work. *Bellows PB-6* (illustrated) has a double-track rail that lets you shift the camera, bellows, and lens as a unit for fine focusing without changing the lens-to-film distance. Lens or camera can also be moved independently. It can also be removed, reversed, and remounted to use the lens in reverse position. Full-aperture viewing and focusing are possible at all times. Magnifications from 1.2X to 3.6X life size are possible with a 50mm lens, magnifications from 1.6X to 4.4X with the lens mounted in reverse. With a 24mm lens, magnification can be as great as 10X.

A slide-copying adapter attaches to a bellows unit for making same-size or enlarged duplicates of 35 mm or smaller slides, negatives, or filmstrips. The adapter also copies 8mm, Super-8, or 16mm film. *Model PS-6* (illustrated) has support trays for uncut rolls and permits cropping by shifting the slideholder 6 mm vertically, 9 mm horizontally.

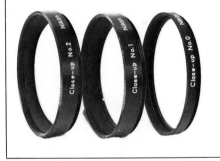

Close-up attachment lenses thread onto the front of any camera lens with a 52mm or 62mm filter thread. They are available in several strengths and can be used individually or in combination. They give their best performance at small lens apertures and are suitable for photographing objects that do not require extreme magnification. Special T-series close-up lenses, designed for use with telephoto lenses, have two-element construction. All of the close-up lenses are coated like other Nikon lenses to reduce reflections and improve color rendition and contrast.

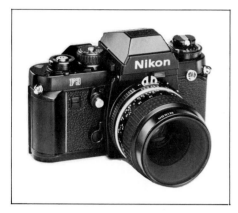

Micro Nikkor lenses are specially designed for close-up work but can also be used for general purpose photography. The 200mm f/4 IF Micro Nikkor lens shown provides continuous focusing from infinity to .5X life size and, when used with the TC-300 Teleconverter, will produce a life-size image. The relatively long lens produces a large image without your having to get extremely close to the subject—a convenience since the lens won't be as likely to block light or to frighten a living subject as a shorter lens used closer to the subject. Other Micro Nikkor lenses include a 55mm f/2.8 and a 105mm f/4.

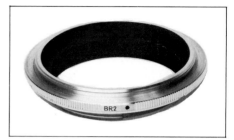

Reversing a lens so the rear element of the lens faces the subject produces better optical performance at very close focusing distances (1X life-size magnifications or larger). *Macro Adapter Ring BR-2* (illustrated) lets you mount a 52mm diameter Nikkor lens in reverse position on extension rings or bellows. *Macro Adapter Ring BR-3* (not shown) converts the bayonet mount of a reverse-mounted lens into a 52mm diameter thread that will accept a filter, lens hood, or slide-copying adapter.

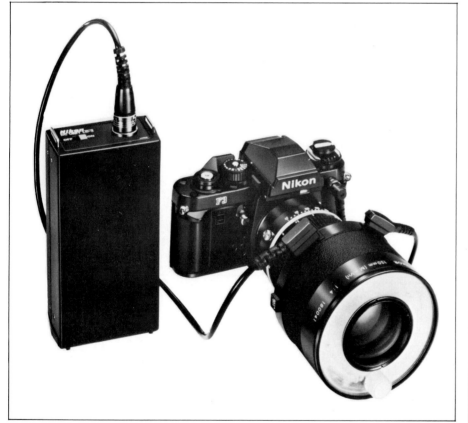

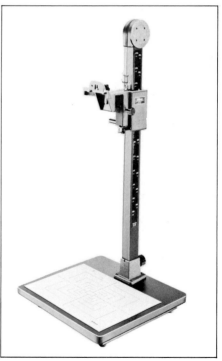

The Medical-Nikkor 120mm f/4 IF lens, shown here with the F3 camera, is a close-up lens originally designed for medical and dental photography, but also used for close-ups and in industrial and scientific applications. Focusing lights and a Xenon ringflash tube are built into the front of the lens. The lens provides magnification from 1/11X to 1X, and up to 2X when the close-up at-tachment lens is added. The correct lens aperture for flash is set automatically and there is a provision for imprinting each frame of film with the magnification ratio. The lens is powered by an external power source: the AC pack LA-2 or the DC pack LD-2 (shown here) may be used. Even inexperienced photographers can make good close-ups with this lens.

The Repro Copy Outfit PF-4 consists of a wooden baseboard and an upright column with a sliding camera mount that has coarse and fine focusing adjustments. Reproduction ratios from 1/14 to 1/2X life size are possible with the 55mm Micro Nikkor lens. An accessory table clamp is available and may be substituted for the baseboard.

General accessories Nikon makes an exceptionally large variety of cases, viewing aids, and other accessories. See your dealer for these and other items.

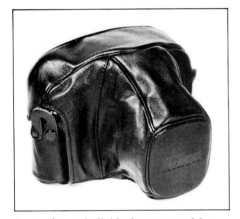

A case for an individual camera and lens protects them against dust, moisture, and accidental damage. A hard case gives the most protection against damage: two-piece eveready construction permits the front of the case to be dropped down so it need not be entirely removed to use the camera. A semisoft case (illustrated) has the same two-piece eveready construction in a more pliable material. A soft case can be folded and put in a pocket when not in use.

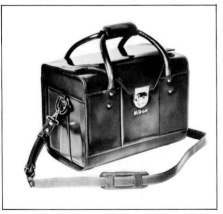

A compartment case holds one or more cameras plus lenses and accessories, and makes equipment easy to transport and store neatly and safely. Each case opens wide so the entire contents are accessible, and the interior is padded and lined. The case shown has a bottom compartment with adjustable, removable partitions for a variety of lenses and accessories, plus a removable tray that holds two cameras (or one plus an extra lens). Nikon makes a variety of case styles.

A lens case (not shown) holds one lens for maximum protection during travel or storage. Hard, cylindrical cases are velveteen-lined and come in various sizes for different lens focal lengths. Larger cases are equipped with shoulder straps. A soft pouch case folds conveniently when not in use. A two-piece plastic case screws together for maximum protection against dust and moisture; the base has a bayonet mount so the lens can be stored without a rear cap. Wooden cases are available for telephoto lenses of 400 mm or longer.

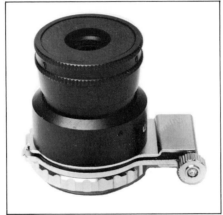

Eyepiece Magnifier DG-2 is particularly useful for close-up photography. It doubles the magnification of the central 12 mm of the viewfinder image for critical focusing and is on a hinged mount so it can be swung up out of the way when not needed. A built-in diopter system corrects for individual eyesight.

A rubber eyecup (not shown) fits around the viewfinder window and makes the viewfinder image easier to see by preventing stray light from entering the window. It also prevents accidental scratching of eyeglass lenses by the viewfinder window or pentaprism. Three types are made for different camera types.

An eyepiece correction lens (not shown) makes viewing and focusing easier if you are nearsighted or farsighted and prefer to photograph without wearing eyeglasses. The lens fits over the viewfinder eyepiece and corrects the viewing image much as eyeglasses do. Several strengths are available.

Right-angle viewing attachment DR-3 makes it easier to view a scene from a low camera angle or when doing copy work. The unit attaches to the viewfinder and can be rotated to the best angle for viewing.

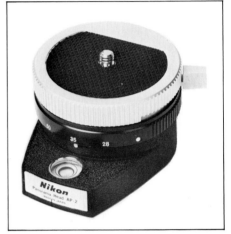

Panorama Head AP-2 connects between the camera and a tripod and simplifies the making of a panorama photograph in which a series of side-by-side images of a scene are made. The head has click-stop positions for precise framing of each shot with 28mm, 35mm, 50mm, 85mm, or 105mm lenses, and may also be used with other lenses. A built-in spirit level helps in aligning the camera.

Nikon international offices

Nippon Kogaku K.K.
Head Office: Fuji Bldg., 2–3,
3-chome Marunouchi
Chiyoda-ku, Tokyo 100
Japan

Overseas subsidiaries:

Nippon Kogaku (U.S.A.) Inc.
623 Stewart Avenue
Garden City, New York 11530
U.S.A.

Nikon Europe B.V.
P.O. Box 7609
1118 ZJ Schiphol Airport
The Netherlands

Nikon AG
Kaspar Fenner-Strasse 6
8700 Küsnacht/ZH
Switzerland

Nikon GmbH
Uerdinger Strasse 96–102
4 Düsseldorf 30
West Germany

GLOSSARY

Prepared by Lista Duren

Aberration Optical defect in a lens (sometimes unavoidable) causing distortion or loss of sharpness in the final image.

Adapter ring A ring used to attach one camera item to another; for example, to attach a lens to a camera in reverse position in order to increase image sharpness when focusing very close to the subject.

Angle of view The amount of a scene that can be recorded by a particular lens; determined by the focal length of the lens.

Aperture The lens opening formed by the iris diaphragm inside the lens. The size is variable and is controlled by the aperture ring on the lens.

Aperture-priority mode An automatic exposure system in which the photographer sets the aperture (f-stop) and the camera selects a shutter speed for correct exposure.

Aperture ring The band on the camera lens that, when turned, adjusts the size of the opening in the iris diaphragm and changes the amount of light that reaches the film.

ASA A number rating that indicates the speed of a film. Stands for American Standards Association.

Auto winder See **Motor drive unit.**

Automatic exposure A mode of camera operation in which the camera automatically adjusts either the aperture, the shutter speed, or both for proper exposure.

Automatic flash An electronic flash unit with a light-sensitive cell that determines the length of the flash for proper exposure by measuring the light reflected back from the subject.

Averaging meter An exposure meter with a wide angle of view. The indicated exposure is based on an average of all the light values in the scene.

Base The supporting material that holds a photographic emulsion. For film, it is plastic or acetate. For prints, it is paper.

Bellows An accordion-pleated section inserted between the lens and the camera body. In close-up photography the bellows allows closer-than-normal focusing resulting in a larger image.

Body The light-tight box that contains the camera mechanisms and protects the film from light until you are ready to make an exposure.

Bounce light Indirect light produced by pointing the light source away from the subject and using a ceiling or other surface to reflect the light back toward the subject. Softer and less harsh than direct light.

Bracketing Taking several photographs of the same scene at different exposure settings, some greater than and some less than the setting indicated by the meter, to ensure a well-exposed photograph.

Built-in meter An exposure meter in the camera that takes a light reading (usually through the camera lens) and relays exposure information to the electronic controls in an automatic camera or to the photographer if the camera is being operated manually.

Cable release An encased wire which attaches at one end to the shutter release on the camera and has a plunger on the other end that the photographer depresses to activate the shutter. Used to avoid camera movement or to activate the shutter from a distance.

Cassette A light-tight metal or plastic container in which 35mm film is packaged.

Center-weighted meter A through-the-lens exposure meter that measures light values from the entire scene but gives greater emphasis to those in the center of the image area.

Close-up A larger-than-normal image obtained by using a lens closer than normal to the subject.

Close-up lens An attachment placed in front of an ordinary lens to allow focusing at a shorter distance in order to increase image size.

Color balance The overall accuracy with which the colors in a color photograph match or are capable of matching those in the original scene. Color films are balanced for use with specific light sources.

Color temperature Description of the color of a light source. Measured on a scale of degrees Kelvin.

Compound lens A lens made up of several lens elements.

Contrast The difference in brightness between the light and dark parts of a scene or photograph.

Contrasty Having greater-than-normal differences between light and dark areas.

Cool Toward the green-blue-violet end of the visible spectrum.

Daylight film Color film that has been balanced to produce natural-looking color when exposed in daylight. Images will look reddish if daylight film is used with tungsten light.

Depth of field The distance between the nearest and farthest points that appear in acceptably sharp focus in a photograph. Depth of field varies with lens aperture, focal length, and camera-to-subject distance.

Diaphragm (iris diaphragm) The mechanism controlling the size of the lens opening and therefore the amount of light that reaches the film. It consists of several overlapping metal leaves inside the lens that form a circular opening of variable sizes. (You can see it as you look into the front of the lens.) The size of the opening is referred to as the f-stop or aperture.

Diffused light Light that has been scattered by reflection or by passing through a translucent material. An even, often shadowless, light.

DIN A number rating used in Europe that indicates the speed of a film. Stands for Deutsche Industrie Norm.

Diopter Unit of measurement that indicates the magnifying power of a close-up lens.

Direct light Light shining directly on the subject and producing strong highlights and deep shadows.

Directional/diffused light Light that is partly direct and partly scattered. Softer and less harsh than direct light.

Electronic flash (strobe) A camera accessory that provides a brilliant flash of light. A battery-powered unit requires occasional recharging or battery replacement, but, unlike a flashbulb, can be used repeatedly.

Emulsion A thin coating of gelatin, containing a light-sensitive material such as silver-halide crystals plus other chemicals, spread evenly on one surface of film or paper to record an image.

Environmental portrait A photograph in which the subject's surroundings are important to the portrait.

Exposure 1. The act of allowing light to strike a light-sensitive surface. 2. The amount of light reaching the film, controlled by the combination of aperture and shutter speed.

Exposure meter (light meter) An instrument that measures the brightness of light and provides aperture and shutter speed combinations for correct exposure. Exposure meters may be built into the camera or they may be separate instruments.

Exposure mode The type of camera operation (such as manual, shutter-priority, aperture-priority) that determines which controls you set and which ones the camera sets automatically. Some cameras operate in only one mode. Others may be used in a variety of modes.

Extension tubes Metal rings attached between the camera lens and the body to allow closer-than-normal focusing in order to increase the image size.

Fill light A light source or reflector used to lighten shadow areas so that contrast is decreased.

Film A roll or sheet of a flexible material coated on one side with a light-sensitive emulsion and used in the camera to record an image.

Film advance lever A device, usually on the top of the camera, that winds the film forward a measured distance so that an unexposed segment moves into place behind the shutter.

Film plane (focal plane) The surface inside the camera on which the image is in sharp focus.

Film speed The relative sensitivity to light of photographic film. Measured by ASA (or ISO or DIN) rating. Faster film (higher number) is more sensitive to light and requires less exposure than slower film.

Filter A piece of colored glass or plastic placed in front of the camera lens to alter the quality of the light reaching the film.

Filter factor A number, provided by the filter manufacturer, that tells you how much to increase exposure to compensate for the light absorbed by the filter. You usually don't have to be concerned with filter factors if your camera has a through-the-lens metering system.

Fisheye lens An extreme wide angle lens covering a 180° angle of view. Straight lines appear curved at the edge of the photograph, and the image itself may be circular.

Flare Stray light that reflects between the lens surfaces and results in a loss of contrast or an overall grayness in the final image.

Flash 1. A short burst of light emitted by a flashbulb or electronic flash unit at the same time the film is exposed. 2. The equipment used to produce this light.

Flashbulb A battery-powered bulb that emits one bright flash of light and then must be replaced.

Flat Having less-than-normal differences between light and dark areas.

Focal length The distance from the optical center of the lens to the film plane when the lens is focused on infinity. The focal length is usually expressed in millimeters (mm) and determines the angle of view (how much of the scene can be included in the picture) and the size of objects in the image. A 100mm lens, for example, has a narrow angle of view and magnifies objects by comparison with a lens of shorter focal length.

Focal plane See **Film plane.**

Focus 1. The point at which the rays of light coming through the lens converge to form a sharp image. The picture is "in focus" or sharpest when this point coincides with the film plane. 2. To change the lens-to-film distance (or the camera-to-subject distance) until the image is sharp.

Focusing ring The band on the camera lens that, when turned, moves the lens in relation to the film plane, focusing the camera for specific distances.

Focusing screen See **Viewing screen.**

Frame 1. A single image in a roll of film. 2. The edges of an image.

Fresnel An optical surface with concentric circular steps. Used in a viewing screen to equalize the brightness of the image.

F-stop (f-number) A numerical designation (f/2, f/2.8, etc.) indicating the size of the aperture (lens opening).

Ghosting Bright spots in the picture the same shape as the aperture (lens opening) caused by reflections between lens surfaces.

Grain The speckled effect caused by particles of silver clumping together in the negative.

Guide number A number on a flash unit that can be used to calculate the correct aperture for a particular film speed and flash-to-subject distance.

Hand-held meter An exposure meter that is separate from the camera.

Hand hold To support the camera with the hands rather than with a tripod or other fixed support.

High-contrast film Film that records light tones lighter and dark tones darker than normal, thereby increasing the difference between tones.

Hot shoe A clip on the top of the camera that attaches a flash unit and provides an electrical link to synchronize the flash with the camera shutter, eliminating the need for a sync cord.

Hyperfocal distance The distance to the nearest object in focus when the lens is focused on infinity. Setting the lens to focus on this distance instead of on infinity will keep the farthest objects in focus as well as extend the depth of field to include objects closer to the camera.

Incident-light meter A hand-held exposure meter that measures the amount of light falling on the subject. See also **Reflected-light meter.**

Indoor film See **Tungsten film.**

Infinity designated ∞. The farthest distance marked on the focusing ring of the lens, generally about 50 feet. When the camera is focused on infinity, all objects at that distance or farther away will be sharp.

Infrared film Film that is sensitive to wavelengths slightly longer than those in the visible spectrum as well as to some wavelengths within the visible spectrum.

Interchangeable lens A lens that can be removed from the camera and replaced by another lens.

Iris diaphragm See **Diaphragm.**

ISO A film speed rating that is replacing the ASA and DIN ratings. Stands for International Standards Organization.

Latitude The amount of over- or underexposure possible without a significant change in the quality of the image.

LED See **Light-emitting diode.**

Lens One or more pieces of optical glass used in the camera to gather and focus light rays to form an image.

Lens cleaning fluid A liquid made for cleaning lenses without damaging the delicate coating on the lens surface.

Lens coating A thin transparent coating on the surface of the lens which reduces light reflections.

Lens element A single piece of optical glass that acts as a lens or as part of a lens.

Lens hood (lens shade) A shield that fits around the lens to prevent extraneous light from entering the lens and causing ghosting or flare.

Lens tissue A soft lint-free tissue made specifically for cleaning camera lenses. Not the same as eyeglass cleaning tissue.

Light-emitting diode (LED) A display of colored lights in the viewfinder of some cameras that gives you information about aperture and shutter speed settings or other exposure data.

Light meter See **Exposure meter.**

Long-focal-length lens (telephoto lens) A lens that provides a narrow angle of view of a scene, including less of a scene than a lens of normal focal length and therefore magnifying objects in the image.

Macro lens A lens specifically designed for close-up photography and capable of good optical performance when used very close to a subject.

Macrophotography Production of images on film that are life-size or larger.

Magnification The size of an object as it appears in an image. Magnification of an image on film is determined by the lens focal length. A long-focal-length lens makes an object appear larger (provides greater magnification) than a short-focal-length lens.

Main light The primary source of illumination.

Manual exposure A nonautomatic mode of camera operation in which the photographer sets both the aperture and the shutter speed.

Match-needle metering A manual exposure mode in which the photographer adjusts the shutter speed and aperture until the camera's viewfinder shows (by matching two needles or by other indicators) that the film will be properly exposed.

Matte Not shiny.

Meter 1. See **Exposure meter.** 2. To take a light reading with a meter.

Mirror A polished metallic reflector set inside the camera body at a 45° angle to the lens to reflect the image up onto the focusing screen. When a picture is taken, the mirror moves so that light can reach the film.

Motor drive unit (auto winder) A camera accessory that automatically advances the film once it has been exposed.

Negative 1. An image with colors or dark and light tones that are the opposite of those in the original scene. 2. Film that was exposed in the camera and processed to form a negative image.

Negative film Photographic film that produces a negative image upon exposure and development.

Neutral density filter A piece of dark glass or plastic placed in front of the camera lens to decrease the intensity of light entering the lens. It affects exposure, but not color.

Normal-focal-length lens (standard lens) A lens that provides about the same angle of view of a scene as the human eye and that does not unduly magnify or diminish the relative size of objects in the image.

Open up To increase the size of the lens aperture. The opposite of stop down.

Orthochromatic film Film that is sensitive to blue and green light but not red light.

Overexposure Exposing the film to more light than is needed to render the scene as the eye sees it. Results in a negative that is too dark (dense) or a positive that is too light.

Pan To move the camera during the exposure in the same direction as a moving subject. The effect is that the subject stays relatively sharp and the background becomes blurred.

Panchromatic film Film that is sensitive to the wavelengths of the visible spectrum.

Pentaprism A five-sided optical device used in an eye-level viewfinder to correct the image from the focusing screen so that it appears right side up and correct left to right.

Perspective The illusion of a three-dimensional space suggested primarily by converging lines and the decrease in size of objects farther from the camera.

Photoflood A tungsten lamp designed especially for use in photographic studios. It emits light at 3400 K and is suitable for use with tungsten Type A film.

Photomicrography Photographing through a microscope.

Polarizing screen (polarizing filter) A filter placed in front of the camera lens to reduce reflections from nonmetallic surfaces like glass or water.

Positive An image with colors or light and dark tones that are similar to those in the original scene.

Print An image (usually a positive one) on photographic paper, made from a negative or a transparency.

Quartz lamp A tungsten lamp which has high intensity, small size, long life, and constant color temperature. Balanced for use with tungsten film.

Reciprocity effect (reciprocity failure) A shift in the color balance or the darkness of an image caused by very long or very short exposures.

Reflected-light meter An exposure meter (hand held or built into the camera) that reads the amount of light reflected from the subject. See also **Incident-light meter.**

Reflector Any surface—a ceiling, a card; an umbrella, etc.—used to bounce light onto a subject.

Reversal film Photographic film that produces a positive image (a transparency) upon exposure and development.

Reversal processing A procedure for producing a positive image on film (a transparency) from the film exposed in the camera or a positive print from a transparency with no negative involved.

Rewind crank A device, usually on the top of the camera, for winding the film back into the cassette once it has been exposed.

Shoe A clip on a camera for attaching a flash unit. See also **Hot shoe.**

Short-focal-length lens (wide-angle lens) A lens that provides a wide angle of view of a scene, including more of the subject area than a lens of normal focal length.

Shutter A device in the camera that opens and closes to expose the film to light for a measured length of time.

Shutter-priority mode An automatic exposure system in which the photographer sets the shutter speed and the camera selects the aperture (f-stop) for correct exposure.

Shutter release The mechanism, usually a button on the top of the camera, that activates the shutter to expose the film.

Shutter speed dial The camera control that selects the length of time the film is exposed to light.

Silhouette A dark shape with little or no detail appearing against a light background.

Single-lens-reflex (SLR) A type of camera with one lens which is used both for viewing and for taking the picture. A mirror inside the camera reflects the image up into the viewfinder. When the picture is taken, this mirror moves out of the way, allowing the light entering the lens to travel directly to the film.

Slide See **transparency.**

SLR See **single-lens-reflex.**

Spectrum The range of radiant energy from extremely short wavelengths to extremely long ones. The visible spectrum includes only the wavelengths to which the human eye is sensitive.

Speed 1. The relative ability of a lens to transmit light. Measured by the largest aperture at which the lens can be used. A fast lens has a larger maximum aperture and can transmit more light than a slow one. 2. The relative sensitivity to light of photographic film. See **Film speed.**

Standard lens See **Normal-focal-length lens.**

Spot meter An exposure meter with a narrow angle of view, used to take a reading from a small portion of the scene being photographed.

Stop 1. An aperture setting that indicates the size of the lens opening. 2. A change in exposure by a factor of two. Changing the aperture from one setting to the next doubles or halves the amount of light reaching the film. Changing the shutter speed from one setting to the next does the same thing. Either changes the exposure one stop.

Stop down To decrease the size of the lens aperture. The opposite of open up.

Stopped-down automatic exposure A mode of operation possible with some cameras. Ordinarily the camera meters the scene (and you view the scene) with the aperture wide open, stopping down to the proper aperture only when the picture is taken. In stopped-down exposure the camera meters the scene with the aperture already stopped down.

Strobe See **Electronic flash.**

Substitution reading An exposure meter reading taken from something other than the subject, such as a gray card of standard darkness or the photographer's hand.

Sync (or synchronization) cord An electrical wire that links a flash unit to a camera's shutter release mechanism.

Synchronize To cause a flash unit to fire while the camera shutter is open.

Telephoto lens See **long-focal-length lens.**

35mm The width of the film used in all the cameras described in this book.

Through-the-lens meter (TTL meter) An exposure meter built into the camera which takes light readings through the lens.

Transparency (slide) A positive image on a clear film base viewed by passing light through from behind with a projector or light box. Usually in color.

Tripod A three-legged support for the camera.

TTL Abbreviation for through the lens, as in through-the-lens viewing or metering.

Tungsten-balanced film Color film that has been balanced to produce colors that look natural when exposed in tungsten light, specifically light of 3200 K color temperature. Images will look bluish if tungsten-balanced film is used in daylight. *Type A tungsten film* has a slightly different balance for use with photoflood bulbs of 3400 K color temperature.

Umbrella reflector An apparatus constructed like a parasol with a reflective surface on the inside. Used to bounce or diffuse light onto a subject.

Underexposure Exposing the film to less light than is needed to render the scene as the eye sees it. Results in a negative that is too light (thin) or a positive that is too dark.

Viewfinder eyepiece An opening in the camera through which the photographer can see the scene to be photographed.

Viewing screen The surface on which the image in the camera appears for viewing. This image appears upside down and reversed left to right unless the camera contains a pentaprism to correct it.

Vignette To shade the edges of an image so they are underexposed. A lens hood that is too long for the lens will cut into the angle of view and cause vignetting.

Visible spectrum See **Spectrum.**

Warm Toward the red-orange-yellow end of the visible spectrum.

Wide-angle distortion Unusual changes in perspective or in the appearance of objects caused by using a wide-angle (short-focal-length) lens very close to the subject.

Wide-angle lens See **Short-focal-length lens.**

Zone focusing Presetting the focus to photograph action so that the entire area in which the action may take place will be sharp.

Zoom lens A lens with several moving elements which can be used to produce a continuous range of focal lengths.

INDEX